WILD PLACES

William Neill

First Edition 1985

WILD PLACES

Poems In Three Leids

By

William Neill

Luath Press LTD.
Barr, Ayrshire.

Other Publications by William Neill:

Scotland's Castle. Reprographia. 1970
Poems. Akros. 1970
Four Points Of A Saltire. Reprographia. 1970
(With Sorley Maclean, Stuart MacGregor and George Campbell Hay)
Despatches Home. Reprographia. 1972
Buile Shuibhne. Club Leabhar. 1974
Galloway Landscape. Urr Publications. 1981
Cnu A Mogaill. Celtic Dept., Glasgow University. 1983

Acknowledgements:
Included in this present collection are some poems which first appeared in the following
publications:
Chapman. Gairm. Lines Review. The Scots Magazine. The Scottish Review.
The Times Educational Supplement. Dumfries and Galloway Standard.

The Publisher acknowledges subsidy from the Scottish Arts
Council towards the publication of this volume.

FEART SULA DHUIT, FEART DULA DHUIT.

Thy Lustye bewte and thy youth
sall feid as dois the somer flouris;
Syne sal the swallow with his mouth
The dragone Death that all devouris.
No castel sall the keip, nor touris,
Bot he sall seik the with thy feiris;
Thairfore, remembir at all houris
quod tu in cinerem reverteris.

William Dunbar (1460–1520)

CONTENTS

INTRODUCTION	1
FOREWORD	5
Wild Places	9
Map Makers	10
Church History	11
Art Lesson	13
Bull	14
Countryman	15
Smeuran An Fhoghair	17
Colonial Service	18
Kailyard and After	19
A Walk On The Hill	20
Dead Farmer	23
Addicts	23
Flies	24
Generation Gap	25
Modern Architecture	25
Drumbarchan Mains	27
Airsair	28
Antiquary	29
Dead Poet's House	31
Hertsaw	32
Gone For A Soldier	33
In Memoriam	34
Airgead Is Ardan	35
Iona	37
Lament For MacGregor O Glenstrae	38
Looking South To The Wall	41
John Roy Stuart	42
I Remember, I Remember	43

Moorland Pylons 45
Simmer Time 45
The Harnpan 46
Mr. Burns For Supper 50
Iona Remains 52
Wild Geese 54
Winter Woodland 55
Olympian Decision 55
The Unknown 56
Timon 57
Cummha Bhaltair Cinneide 58
In Memory Of Walter Kennedy 59
Song To The Highland Dress 61
The Auld Grunn 62
The Old Croft 63
Sirens 64
Edders And Aipples 67
Old Soldier 68
Vision 69
Posthumous Fame 69
Religious Instruction 70
Worldly Aims 71
Spring Drowning 72
September Sheaves 72
Sheep 73
Morning Frost 73
Social Change 74
Power 75
May Day 75
Man Walking 76
Kierkegaard 76
Spider Story 77
Lark 78
Distance 78
A Knell For Mr. Burns 79
Landscapes 80
Yellow Charlie Gunn 81
Homewards 82
Evolution 83
Erncrogo 84

Death Of The Technical Missionary 85
Dante 86
Convert 87
Blithe Spirit 88
Autumn Light 89
Bards 90
Archilochus 92
Dispossessed Poet 93
I Intended A Sonnet 94
Iliad 95
Inque Brevi Spatio Mutantur 96
Modern Biography 98
Nicholas Herman 99
Non-Academic Group 100
The Place For Poetry 101
Scapegoat 101
Rural Bard 102
Poetry Lesson 103
Scarecrow 105
Shrink 106
Teacher 106
Unpublished Poets 107
Inde Cadunt Mortes 108
History Lesson 109
Art And Salvation 110
Envoi To The Dean's Book 112
Faur Ahint Maun Follow Faster 114
Exile 117
Viewpoint 118
Findabar's Song 118
Dance 119
Taliesin: A Strathclyde Winter 120
Beach Walking 122
Sermon On Mid Lent Sunday 123
Exodus 127
The Poet's House 128
Maya In The Garden 128
Rustic Squalor 129
Second Wedding 129
Scotia Est Divisa In Voces Tres 130

First Love 133
Orphan 133
Metanoia 134
Old Enemies 134
A Question For Experts 135
Skeletons 135
Political Systems 136
The Isle Of Innis-Chanter 138
Armed Intervention 140
Modern Hubris 140
Who Won? 141
Ballant 142
Three Men In A Wood 143
Drought 143
The Fickle Finger Of Fame 144
The Turned Furrow 145
On The Appointment Of A Poet Laureate ...146
Summer Visitation 148
In His Own Country 152
Forced March 152
Nature 153
Drinks 153
Listed House: Stewartry 155
Nursemaids And Soldiers 156
Frame 156
Lochar Watter 157
Memo. To Chris. Grieve 159
Wha Jeedges Pigs,
Jeedges Sculpture Tae 162

A Packet Of Broadsheets

Sawnie's Complaint 164

Crionadh Foghlam Na H-Alba
Or: The Crynan O Scotia's Lear
Or: The Decline Of Scottish Learning 170

Another Letter To Lord Byron 177

The Jolly Trimmers
Or: Love Of Slavery 187

INTRODUCTION

It will come as a surprise to some that this sixth collection of William Neill's poetry consists mainly of work in English — rather than in Scots or Gaelic (though both these languages are represented in the book). Neill is best known to the Scottish reading public, after all, as a patriotic polemicist and as an exponent of modern Gaelic culture. In the first capacity he once edited *Catalyst*, the organ of the radical *1320 Club,* and now frequently expresses his opinions in incisive letters to *The Scotsman*. In 1969 he made headlines when he gained the Bardic Crown at the Aviemore Mod, since the press found it remarkable that a Lowland Scot should have acquired a mastery of Gaelic. Neill, however, believes that the linguistic divisions of Scotland have been imposed politically, that Gaelic is a cultural phenomenon accessible to all Scots, and that it makes artistic sense to write in English as well as Scots and Gaelic because *'this is still the linguistic reality of the Scottish situation.'*

Born in Prestwick in 1922, Neill moved to Ayr at the age of five. He joined the RAF in 1938, served first as a fitter then as a navigator; when he left the RAF in 1967 he held the rank of Warrant Officer. In 1967 Neill went to Edinburgh University as a mature student ('very mature' is his own description) who graduated in 1971 with honours in Celtic Studies. He subsequently taught English, in Galloway, for ten years, then retired (in Castle Douglas) 'to live frugally on vegetables grown by wife and wine fermented by self'.

Neill's poetry is a direct expression of his personality. Never evasive or obscure, he is forceful even in reflection. His poem *'Inde Cadunt Mortes'* begins, characteristically, with an observation of an actual scene before reaching out to an emphatic conclusion:

> While rabbits, like their betters, take no heed
> but risk swift death for a mere whimsy's sake,
> Mankind to mankind less indifference shows:
> we kill for spite as well as feeding crows.

These lines suggest the themes that most concern Neill. There is an insight into the life of the countryside, an obsession with the omnipresence of death, a moralistic revulsion with the inhumanity of humankind. Neill is, in a very positive manner, a didactic poet who writes always with passion and often with indignation.

As a child Neill was (as he told me) 'conversant with all the work and life of a small Ayrshire farm in the days of horses, men and hands rather than machines'. His poems begin with the assumption that a rural community is spiritually superior to urban chaos. In *'Countryman'* he distances himself from the 'city's rush' and rejoices that his 'gable rubs no other tenement'. In *'The Old Croft'* he comes back to the countryside, glad to be apart from 'the choking towns'. *'Man Walking'* opens with the image of a man coalescing with the countryside:

> On the hill-slope man merges into trees,
> loses particular, melts to stone and grass
> where following breezes lend him a swift ease
> as he strides on past all so all things pass.

Neill thus sounds the theme of rural retreatism which is so prevalent in modern poetry, especially that associated with Celts. Yeats, remember, wanted to rise and go to his bee-loud glade, Dylan Thomas equated Eden with the days when he was young and easy among the apple boughs, Edwin Muir spent his creative life in an eternal escape from the inferno he experienced in Glasgow, Hugh MacDiarmid dismissed Scotland's two biggest cities as 'rubbish'. Neill uses the rural theme in a distinctive way, to give a natural dimension to his urgent evocations of death. In his countryside, death is seen in the context of the perennial cycle of the seasons. So Neill writes, in *'The Turned Furrow'*:

> My field was tilled and my seed sown,
> I saw the stalks of my harvest bend,
> but I got nothing but stiff bones
> and a grey head at the day's end.

It is, of course, inevitable that beings as sensitive as poets will reflect on death in general. Neill, though, dwells on his own death as if he expected it at any moment. 'Now my time's very nearly run', he writes in *'Lark'* while in *'I Remember, I Remember'* he speaks of 'my dying bodies muddle-mettled ground'. Readers of this book will surely find, as I did, that Neill writes movingly about old age and death and will welcome his ability to embrace what is a notoriously difficult subject. Neill has lived with the facts of death for most of his life: his mother died one year after his birth and during World War Two friends of his were killed in action. Neill's poetry confronts the ontological implications of death, perhaps most impressively in *'Sermon on Midlent Sunday'* which opens ominously:

> Think when you rise: this day may be your last.
> In this night's sleep daylight might never come.

For all his interest in death, Neill writes with great vitality about the anomalies of contemporary society. Obviously he cares deeply about the survival of the human race, so puts a fine satirical edge on some of his metrical comments on those who would destroy the culture he believes in preserving. Neill's discursive poems show an adroit command of rhyme; indeed, all his poems are well crafted. Evidently he believes in structurally sound poems and in the virtues of formal verse. Technically a traditionalist, he can turn a moral issue into a memorable couplet or quatrain.

Neill is a prolific poet who has learned his craft from various sources yet retained his individuality. When he writes in Scots or

3

Gaelic he shows a close familiarity with the work of great modern masters such as MacDiarmid and Sorley Maclean. Neill's English verse, it seems to me, has an ironic anger reminiscent of the war poems of Siegfried Sassoon. Given his criticisms of the Scottish people, Neill has a Hardyesque faith in their ability to endure.

I have indicated that Neill is a didactic poet, yet there is nothing academic or institutional about his approach; he wraps up his message in an attractive linguistic package. Neill has descriptive flair, a countryman's appreciation of natural beauty, an eye for pictorially sharp images, an admirable intellectual clarity. His best poems exhibit, too, a hint of mystery as if acknowledging that even the author does not know all the answers. Read the first stanza of 'The Unknown' and notice how the poem operates on several levels so that the subject of the first stanza could be a ghost or God or something more mundane:

> When the unknown began to rattle and bang
> immoderately in the empty room upstairs;
> when, as if tipsy, it obscenely sang,
> they blacked it out with everyday affairs.

Like so many of Neill's poems, that one makes the reader think. Personally I find William Neill one of the most stimulating and entertaining of living Scottish poets, and am convinced that this book is his finest achievement to date.

ALAN BOLD

FOREWORD

I cannot recall having written anything about my own work before, so I have accepted Tom Atkinson's suggestion that I do so here.

It will be seen that I pay no attention to the idea that poetry should not be polemical, didactic or rhetorical; or that anything to which such adjectives can be applied cannot be poetry. The history of literature is against such a view.

I live in the countryside and write a great deal about it. It is where most men on this island lived just over two centuries ago. The great urban warren is a modern phenomenon. I am not a townie sentimentalist about rural life; I have *skailt sharn* and stooked corn, and I am as familiar with the stinks of the countryside as its scents.

I make verses about death. Apart from pain, which I fear as much as any person of sense, the prospect of my own death interests rather than disturbs me. I do not write such poems from a sense of impending doom. Either dreamless sleep, or better conversation, said Socrates; to me, Pascal's wager seems a good bet. Not to think about death is not to think about life, of which our passing is a major feature. I write about death as a fitting antidote to the almost psychotic selfishness of an affluence concerned only with the scratching of its own itches in the illusion that such mindless titillation can be extended indefinitely by purchase. I am, however, not an advocate of haggard puritanism.

I have read a great deal of poetry in the Celtic tongues. Formal stanzas, clear images and a lack of obscurity are the characteristics of its best exemplars; Celtic mistiness is an invention of non-Celts and bad romantic novelists. It is this 'bright' poetry which is to my own taste and I hope it has influenced my own work. While difficult language may be necessary for subtle notions, opacity as a disguise for dullness ought to be discouraged. I try to benefit from Coleridge's opinion that poetry must be more than good sense but dare not be less.

I like to use all the gadgets in the poetic workshop; to throw these in the dustbin in the interests of alleged artistic progress is like dismantling a car, scrapping all its locomotive parts and pointing to the remaining heap as an advance in road transport.

There are a few poems in Gaelic and Scots in this book. Scots I got in the fields of my youth, standard English I got in the classroom, Gaelic I made a point of acquiring. Gaelic was spoken in Ayrshire for a thousand years, disappearing round about 1700, and is still vigorous in north-west Scotland. A little family history and elementary arithmetic prove that my ancestors spoke it. Scots is still alive in the southwest of Scotland, and I delight in its pure vowels, German fricatives, and clear Norse consonants. There are macaronic poems in Gaelic and Scots; I am not the first Ayrshireman to write such verses — Alexander Montgomerie beat me by about four hundred years.

I deprecate the increasing acceptance by simple-minded snobs of the idea that only the attitudes, allophones and lexis germane to the area south and east of Pangbourne are socially or intellectually acceptable. Only recently a London critic reproved a Scottish writer for the use of the word *thole*, which is still in common use in Scotland (and northern England). Did not Shakespear delight in the sound of strange words? A more perceptive critic, Kathleen Raine, pointed out that it was inclination rather than difficulty which kept English readers from Scots poetry. (*AGENDA* Vol 9 No. 2–3). Creative writers should not allow themselves to be pushed into a barren lexical or stylistic aridity.   One may ask if the same critic would object to the American *'gotten'*.

From its conception to the last draft, the making of a poem is absorbing to the poet.   But that is not the end of the matter, for a poem is not complete until it is available for others to hear or read.   Here they are, then; if the reader finds in them something of the stimulus that prompted me to write them, the process is complete, and I am content.

WILLIAM NEILL

WILD PLACES

WILD PLACES

They who are used to walking the wild places
are not to be driven mad by a raven's croak,
the beak that stabs the carrion's last traces,
the mistletoe that sucks life from the oak.

The dead lamb's maggots meet with a calm eye;
acorns are strewn before the oak-tree's fall.
Among the rocks wherein the corpses lie
the rising-trumpet is the raven's call.

MAP MAKERS

When Irongray grew out of *Earran Reidh*
the culture could not stand on level ground.
Grey dominies of unmalleable will
invented newer legends of their own
to satisfy the blacksmith and his children.

After *Cill Osbran* closed up to Closeburn
more books were shut than Osbran's psalter.
Seeking to baptize the new born name
the pedants hurried to the nearest water
which wasn't even warm.

When *Seann Bhaile* swelled to Shambelly
the old steading became a glutton's belch.
Every tourist pointed a magic finger
padding lean Fingal to a flabby Falstaff.

The cold men in the city
who circumscribe all latitude
wiped their bullseye glasses
laid down the stabbing pens
that had dealt the mortal wounds
slaying the history of a thousand years
in the hour between lunch and catching the evening train.

————◦————

Earran Reidh: The level ground.
Cill Osbran: The Church of Osbran (or Osbern)
Seann Bhaile: The Old Steading.

These are all Gaelic place names in Southwest Scotland, where Gaelic survived until c.1700. (See Journal of Scottish Studies Vol 17.) Our modern map-makers have Anglicized and bastardized these, and many others.

CHURCH HISTORY

Recall the roofless kirk where Ringan prayed,
the bones of singers in the ancient yard.
After the smashing zealots locked the gate
where superstitious ghosts might keep their ward

still beehive monks chant a goidelic lay
in the dark nave of schooled imagination;
a contrast to the elders' tailored grey
defining bounds to transubstantiation.

Pulpit direction marks what is, is not:
decently keeps a subtler darkness hid.
The older mysteries are more surely caught
behind this crumbling wall and bolted grid.

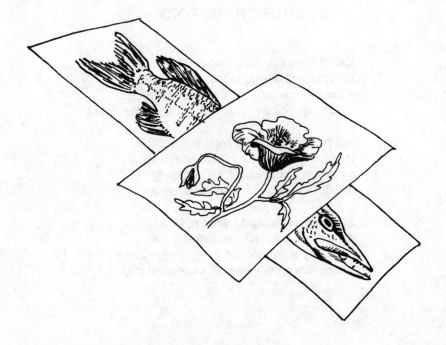

ART LESSON

This boy draws a fish,
captures the cruel pike-jaw and cold eye,
the colours fresh as when he saw it lie
and reached down with a seeking hand to find
its colours in the dark deep of the mind.

This girl draws a flower
so delicate I try to catch its scent
or see its fading with the passing hour.
Her hand's intent
gathered the flower from her inner green
that in my duller eye it might be seen.

Such visions as their inner voices guide
presage some future date
when such clear impulse may be pushed aside,
the fish's form and brightness never seen;
some inner dark blot out the flower-dream.

BULL

The black bull grumbles at me as I pass,
glossy in noonday sunshine, lashing flies
from his tight rump, and rolling his small eyes.
His nose ring marks him of a higher class
than eunuch brethren of the bullock mass
to whom ungoverned lust for beef denies
the tyrant urge that in his members lies.
His flesh is fire and grass to their mere grass.

In this red heat, none of his munching wives
flaunts her desire beneath his wrinkling nose.
He growls and stamps beside the drystone dyke
to put us all in terror of our lives.
But the wall's firm enough. I stop and pose,
a coward matador to his trapped might.

COUNTRYMAN

I walk in greenwoods that they never see;
stride over moor and through the heather bush.
I am the native son, untrammeled, free,
my pace protected from their city's rush.

I take my food from water, blood and earth;
my gable rubs no other tenement,
nor does the city's market weigh my worth;
my measures are the rock and firmament.

Though their soul smothers in the city's pall
their fathers' bones are laid in country graves
where fields lie green outwith their crumbling wall.
Is it my fault that they bide poor, and slaves?

SMEURAN AN FHOGHAIR

Is iomadh bliadhna chaidh seachad
bhon a leig mi dhiom geimhlean na h-oige.
Ach an diugh fhein taobh a chnuic
spion mi smeuran an fhoghair
is ruith an sugh purpaidh air mo bhial.
Chuimhnich mi smeuran eile,
is gu h-obann, bilean eile.

Ach an sin dh'aithnich mi
cha robh caochladh air bith
eadar smeuran an diugh is an de,
oir tha e ceadaichte dhuinn
am blasadh aig an aon am.

BERRIES OF AUTUMN (Translation.)

Many a year has gone past
since I cast off the fetters of youth.
But this very day beside the knowe
I plucked the berries of autumn
and the purple juice ran on my mouth.
I remembered other berries,
and suddenly, other lips.

But then I realised
that there was no difference
between the berries of today and yesterday,
for it is allowed to us
to taste them at the same time.

COLONIAL SERVICE

After due time I became in my own despite
trained to their skills, thirled to their petty wars.
No open bloody tournament of Mars
but a steely guardianship of distant might
whose laws I took for mine, whose right my right.
For I thought: these are the great who house and feed me;
theirs then the right in life to scourge and bleed me.

So I patrolled the walls of an ancient town,
clinked harness in the narrow shaded street,
tramping a conquered rage beneath my feet
when for their rule I aped my captain's frown,
making their scholar equal to their clown.
Clothed by *esprit* in our great arrogance
founded on fortune put to the weapon's chance.

Grew to be of their town but not of their kind;
loving their women, drinking in their inns,
laughed with their worthies at our common sins.
Ruling them, yet half-twisted to their mind
forgot the mountains I had left behind;
forgot their smiling masked a longing hate
that looked for rust upon our iron state.

Then, my time gone too soon, returning home
with the heart heavy, loving the land we left,
like a long-wed man of a good wife bereft.
We set our eyes again toward spire and dome
of that great city whence our troop had come.
Faded the fondness for native glen and stream,
soul-scorched for the land where my strong years had been.

KAILYARD AND AFTER

Whan I wes wee I hud tae dae ma share
mulkan the kye wi the weemin in the byre;
I mind hou I wad scoosh lang streeman jaups
that loupit in the luggie makkin froth
rise oot frae yon rich deeps.

The douce kye skelpit roon thaim wi their tails
tae dicht the flees aff: whiles they'd cotch yir lug
a fair bit ding: ye'd sweir ablo yir braith.
An whiles the wilder yins wad try tae pit
their fit intil the luggie and caa ye oot
on tae the settles, luggie, stuil an aa....
an gin ye didna set in ticht eneuch
there ye wad be, rubbin a sair hainch
a loch o mulk aboot ye in the grup,
the auld dug barkan and the weemin lauchan
tae see yir breeks aa smoort wi mulk and sharn.

Man, whit a contrast tae ma life-style nou.....
nae dungarees, nae luggie and nae kye.

Escape to the tailored suit,
the pan-loaf speech,
the benefits of higher education,
the dull rewards of strict conformity.

O what a fall was there, my countrymen.

---

scoosh: squirt. *jaups:* heavy drops. *loupit:* leapt. *luggie:* a milking
pail. *douce:* easy-going. *skelpit:* smacked. *lug:* ear. *caa:*
propel. *hainch:* haunch. *grup:* dung-channel. *sharn:* cow-dung.
kye: cows.

A WALK ON THE HILL

Walking on the hill's the only thing worth while
after the Sunday papers, London style
journalism that tries to take the place
of vanished rituals, but lacks their grace.
It is not likely that the great will care
for old men's brooding over things long gone:
old faiths, old tongues, the runes we leaned upon.
Grazing sheep are the only audience here.

Wordsworth wandered under wheeling plovers,
boomed behind trees to frighten rural lovers.
He knew the ghost that lived in rock and thorn,
could not escape the groves, being druid-born.
We do not have his audience to share
his cadences, start from his common ground
to sense the deeps that lie beneath the sound.
Where are they gone who once had ears to hear?

They are hard at work on urban confrontation
at levels fitting to their rank and station,
not to be seen here in this empty land
of sloping rigs, hawthorn on either hand.
In my lone head I hear the antique reasons
for sky and water, rock and thorn and cloud,
the road that leads from naked birth to shroud,
flesh divided into seven seasons.

--->

Each seven years they say a man's renewed
from head to toe.   With what are we imbued
that holds our dying substances in one
from our first suck until the whole thing's done
and all our dust and moisture split and spread?
Some secret otherness than flesh and bone
that links the child to age when cells are gone:
the hidden ghost of soul and heart and head.

Alembic to electron microscope,
in all their science not a meagre hope
that they can formulate the unseen mist
that into our more solid flesh is pressed;
a shade no man-made gear can mark or trace,
a flash caught only in the mystic mind
when reason's calculation's left behind;
for there's no law or logic fits the case.

The ram that moves within the thicket there
covers his mistress with no courtly air.
A mouth and bowel motion: oestrogen
dictates his lust.   Unlike the way of men
who of their procreation make a game
played out in joy or pain as falls the case.
With no more eye towards the future race
we give the ram's task a poetic name.

The beasts that move upon the hillside here
are moved by herdlife, hunger, lust and fear.
I wonder all cannot see man's clear case
lies beyond this poor gift in granted grace.
It is the moving spirit that makes man
the sole possessor of clear thought and choice:
arrangement, pattern, altruism's voice,
great art and memory and soul and plan.

———>

In fleshly procreation egg and seed
march down the centuries to make the breed,
but we are bound by other, unseen chains,
for when the bone is dust, this wraith remains.
Today I walk in step with it on the hill;
the unseen pacing of another walker
who fills the silence with a kind of talking.
When I am coffined, I may walk here still.

For it is not mere flesh, mere blood and bone
crushes this grass and stumbles on this stone,
but all things linked to one, yet separate;
a one-not-one with a much greater state
in which upon this hill I join and part
as the mind fills and ebbs with every step.
By rock and root and drystone dyke and slap
the stillness of true knowledge fills the heart.

Now in still hope down from the hill again,
back to the weary cities of the plain
that in their complications ape the beast;
make, for all knowledge, false gods of the least.
Traherne knew all about the Landlord's will:
the great heritage that stretches to the rim
of vision or the reach of willing limb.
All that's worth while is walking on the hill.

DEAD FARMER

Today without labour he goes through his fields again.
There will be no late return to the wholesome meal.
A mark or two of his industry remain
in the tended steading and the growing field.

The earth in which he is planted will grow and seed;
the seed will fly on the prevailing wind
to sow new acres with his living bread.
His followers shall eat of their own kind.

Of the part that spoke within he leaves no trace,
his kingdom's marches joined to some further land.
Those who are left scan both grounds in his place,
hoping to further the same ends that he planned.

ADDICTS

At those who walk forth from prayer and confession
junkie and lush look out from their Sunday panes.
The spirit that clasps them tight in his possession
is not pried off by memories that remain
of other vital essences, once plain,
now misted over as bygone superstition,
the jailer of the soul, the body's prison.

Spiritual sustenance, since God is dead
they seek anew under an altered name:
exorcism for the bleak phantoms bred
in the bleak wilderness of the broken dream.
With grosser numen they thrill the flowing vein
raise manic paradise on ghostly peaks
falling to dry water-courses where the heart breaks.

FLIES

Scenting my sweat run free in the still heat
as if I were a corpse the flies buzz round;
by them, it seems, no difference is found
between my flesh and the moor's carrion meat.
Mutton's a mere knife-edge beyond the bleat
and death a subtle absence of all sound,
a change from just above to under ground
where none are snubbed or favoured by the leet.

Still, the road's grand under this July sun
that tans my hide as tough 's a leather purse.
Though flies and sweat give rise to graveyard thought
perhaps I'll make it till this long day's done.
Maggots can wait until my meat turns worse
than it's gone yet under my lifetimes's rot.

GENERATION GAP

Doubtless when he bent down to pick up
pebbles, and to snatch a quick look round,
he heard the old men growling: *Cheeky pup,*
seconds before Goliath hit the ground.

So, son, the day you undertake
the local giant's precipitate removal,
do it, by all means, for society's sake.
But don't expect your Dad's help.   Or approval.

MODERN ARCHITECTURE

Built in grandfather's day the fountain's dry.
Neither water nor wine, highdays and holidays.
In buried stones some future dig may pry
to discover that generation's unsavoury ways.
Now that we know so well how hygiene pays
the piazza's paved with concrete, the windows blind;
no blackhearted superstitions haunt the mind.

There are no brutes fouling the yard but that feral cat
as thin as an evening kipper's discarded bones;
no pigeons or starlings left to defile your hat;
no ugly lichen growing between the stones,
no nightmare gothic bells to spoil repose,
no bleakhouse graveyards disturb with their ominous sod
now that the functional's rid us of nature and God.

DRUMBARCHAN MAINS

There's monie a nicht I sate in the ingle-neuk
up et Drumbarchan whan I'd taen ma fee,
the rettlin wunnocks jinin in the crack.....
ye cud hae yir telly onie day fur me.

Tae faa asleep in yon bothie, bien and quait
binna the auld meer champin her yeukie heels.
I needit nae het hap tae warm ma feet
nor peels fur a lown belly eftir meals.

Nou there's nae horse tae be fund aboot the ferm
but a muckle rid tractor ahint the stable door
syne auld-sons frae their faithers needna learn
tae ken the fur-ahint frae the lan-afore.

Yince I gaed back tae tak a letter there;
the wife hersel wes loupan roon in breeks.....
no dungarees, ye ken, but velvet claith.....
her dowp wes gey near burstin thro the steeks.

The youngsters tell me that I'm no jist wice,
tae girn at progress, but there's ae thing plain:
Drumbarchan.....Goad! I dinna ken the place.....
hell mend me gin I gang yon gate again.

taen ma fee: been hired.   *rettlin wunnocks:* rattling windows.
jinin in the crack: joining in the talk.   *binna:* except.   *meer:* mare.
bien an quait: comfortable and quiet.   *het hap:* heated blanket.
yeukie: itchy.   *peels:* pills.   *lown:* free of wind.   *steeks:* stitches.
auld-son: eldest son.   *loupan:* jumping.   *dowp:* backside.
fur-ahint, lan-afore: positions of horses in yoke.   *yince:* once.
wice: wise (rhymes with 'dice').   *girn:* complain.   *ae:* one ('yay').
gang yon gate: Go that way.   *gin:* if (hard 'g').

ARSAIR

'Na mo sheasamh an seo ag amharc air cuithean
'nan laighe fhathast air taobh Meall Liath
is sneachd mar chrun ri maol a' Chuirn,
tha ainm gach taigh is cnuic 'nam inntinn,
mar chagar failteach beul Tim.

Is gann a tha fios aig an fhear seo
is e tionndadh chlais le tractair,
air ainm an aite aige fhein
ach mar fhuaim neonach 'na chluais.

Agus nam bithinn 'ga theagaisg,
dh'eisdeadh e le foighidinn
ri cabaireachd a' bhodaich
mun do chuir e sios a chas,
a' sporadh eich gun mhathair
air falbh bho a leithid de sheanachas.

Tha crodh na mointich a' coimhead orm.
Is uasal an sloinntearachd acasan,
is tha iad a' geumnaich gu h-ard
an canain an sinnsre.

——>

ANTIQUARY (Translation)

Standing here, looking at the drifts
lying yet on the side of Millyea,
and the snow like a crown on bald Cairnsmore
the name of every house and hill is in my mind,
like a welcoming whisper in the mouth of time.

This fellow here does not know,
and he turning furrows with a tractor,
the name of his own place
except as a curious noise in his ear.

And if I were to teach him
he would listen patiently to the greybeard's gossip,
before he put down his foot
to spur his motherless horse
away from such chatter.

The moorland cattle watch me.
Noble is their ancestry,
and they bellow loudly
in the tongue of their ancestors.

<---

DEAD POET'S HOUSE

In formal setting of this square stone cage
his last phylacteries are neatly stored:
brown under glass the handwriting displayed
faded and still beside the printed word.
Tourists make pilgrimage; their children, bored,
shuffle upon the silence of a room
where only the guide's monotone presumes.

Caged now dead sister's shade with phantom wife
in the grey room, no place for the exotic
long disclaimed sweetheart of the buried life;
bold revolution's smothered and forgotten
in this austerity sheltered from crag and forest.
Late autumn showers hammer on the pane
quenching the mountain-fire and mystic flame.

Mile after mile a drumbeat in the head
booms behind drystone walls in midnight dark.
Abandon all to find true wine, true bread,
essence under symbol, form beneath the rock
holding to the vision of mind beneath the mask.
Then looming rock and flower and running scree
lost in the flickering fire of domesticity.

Returned at evening, high on all magnificence,
having seen from the dalehead a world lie at his feet;
then, wifely patience, the close wild sister, tense
with all suppression; the weird evening meal,
teacups and fairycups, acorns, the seeming real
drowning the real. The great head weaving spells
far from this dull room armoured against the fells.

HERTSAW

Ye're a byornar scunner
deleerit and rouch,
stauchran hame et midnicht,
faa'n doon i the sheuch.

Whit fur ye're no coortin
we an ee tae get mairrit
on the dochter o yon fairm
wi nae sons tae inherit?

Yon yin thet refuised ye
has aidled yir harns;
tak saw fir a sair hert:
kye and weel-biggit barns.

The morn whan yir heid stouns
and dings lik a smiddy,
tak tent whit I tellt ye
and wad muckle Biddy.

Hertsaw: Heart balm. *scunner:* object of disgust.
stauchran: staggering. *sheuch:* ditch. *harns:* brains.
kye: cows. *stouns:* thumps. *smiddy:* smithy.

GONE FOR A SOLDIER

I came from what they thought a godforsaken region
high among barren rock and mountain manners.
They grinned when I sought to join their famous legion
with its drums and armour plate and hoisted banners,
miniscule pay, sour drink and pigsty dinners.
But I was mad for some way of escape
from high unending hills and the herding of sheep.

I never thought, seated on long hill slopes
that there could be a way of life even duller than that;
who had assumed it beyond my highest hopes
to get down from the climb, walk easy on the flat
fertile cornland.   A tribesman forever caught
in the endless breeding-cycle of the herd
and the gossip of men without polish in their words.

I found nothing here but high noses and stiff spines
on the promoted lowly and the privileged high,
teaching the yokel blockheads to form lines,
to trail and to port, to stand to and stand by,
to fasten a web of straps in the proper way.
From a free man among shepherds I became a slave
caught in the relentless clan of the mindless brave.

So now, when not stamping about in the steely eye
of that tough shining veteran with the acid smile
or sweating under gear, aching in shoulder and thigh,
trudging in hard boots mile after thirsty mile,
my heart yearns for the hills, for the rocky defile,
the bleat of sheep, the rattle of horn and hoof,
and I grieve before sleeping, under an alien roof.

IN MEMORIAM

Lord Alfred's inmost soul, shocked by the shades
dragged out by Mr. Darwin from the ground,
grim flesh laid upon patterns found by spades,
or borne by monsters on volcanic mounds.
Those creeping, growling, rending, tearing things
the ugly ancestors of priests and kings?

Hallam was torn by history, toothed and clawed.
All the old straitlaced stories cast away
on Galapagos ground; what had been God,
ophidian chill on the Victorian day.
A too facile dismissal of the essence
gave to dull clay an overweening presence.

Being denied the grace of later light,
he tortured memory with a classroom Nature;
confused the eye's banality with sight,
with horrid accident replaced the creature;
recast the shaman in the role of thief
and buried faith within the shroud of grief.

AIRGEAD IS ARDAN

Feasgar is mi 'nam shuidhe 'san taigh-osd
choinnich mi fear a thuirt gur e bard a bh' ann.
Thug mi dha drama 's dh' eisd mi ris a bhosd,
is aodach na bochdainn air bho chas gu ceann.

Dh'ol e a shath, is co ach mise a phaigh e
is dh' innis e dhomhsa le fanaid, 'na dhol a muigh:
airgead 'nad phoc' chan ann ach plaighe.....
tha sar ulaidh eadar mo dha chluais.

MONEY AND PRIDE *(Translation.)*

One night as I sat in the inn
I met a man who said he was a poet.
I gave him a dram and listened to his boasting
and a beggar's rags on him from head to foot.

He drank his fill, and who but me that paid for it,
and mockingly he told me as he went:
money in your pocket's nothing but a nuisance,
I have real treasure between my two ears.

IONA

Princes once came here in the hope of dying
on sacred ground.   Their markers and bones are lying
in secrecy now under the holy turf,
save for those images thrown with reforming zeal
into the wide embrace of the clasping sea
to thole the eternal requiem of the surf.

When we recover, and look into our hearts
we may choose once more to return to these druid parts;
to think of the broken prince and the long exile,
his soul aching for the abbey in the wood
until a newer, firmer consolation stood
between his darkness in light and the world's guile.

LAMENT FOR MACGREEGOR O GLENSTRAE:
Frae the Gaelic.

(The chronicle o the Vicar o Fortingall: 1570.   The vj da of Apryill Gregor MacGregor of Glensra heddyt at Belloch anno sexte an ten yeris.)

Richt blithe upo yon Lammas morn
my luve and I did play,
but my puir hert wi dule wes worn
afore the bricht noonday.

Cursit the lairdlings and their freens
wha brocht me til this grief,
wha cam in traison tae my luve
and twined him lik a thief.

My een wad neer hae shed thir tears
nor wad thy sire be deid,
gif there had been twal clansmen here
wi Greegor et their heid.

His hause laid on an aiken clug,
his bluid skailt on the grun;
hid I a bicker of yon bluid
fain wad I drink it doun.   (‡)

Wad my ain sire a leper wir,
Grey Colin seik wi plague
The Ruthven lassie wringan haunds
aside whaur they wir laid.

(‡) *cf. the auld tale of Deirdre and Naoise.*

——>

38

Grey Colin and Black Duncan baith
sae ticht I'd twine in airns
wi ilka Campbell in Taymooth
weel happit roon in chains.

Upo the green o Taymooth Tour
in wanrest I wad staund,
nae lock unruggit on my heid
nor skin upon my haund.

O gin I had the laverock's flicht
bauld Greegor's virr abune,
the tapmost stanes of Taymooth Tour
I'd caa doun til the grun.

Their wives are happit snug et hame
sleepan the nicht awa:
by my ain bed I bide my lane
until the daylicht daw.

Fain wad I be wi Greegor there
in muir and birk alane,
than beddit wi the Laird of Dall
in waas o aislar stane.

—–>

Fain hud I been wi Greegor
in an orra sark o hair,
than weiran silk and velvet
wi the Laird of Dalach there.

Ba hu, ba hu, my son forfairn
sae weirdless and sae smaa
I fear ye'll tine the tid, my bairn,
o vengeance on thaim aa.

Dule: grief. *twined:* bound. *hause:* neck.
aiken clug: oaken block. *skailt:* scattered. *airns:* irons.
wanrest: unrest. *unruggit:* unpulled. *laverock:* lark.
virr: strength. *caa doun:* knock down. *happit:* wrapped.
muir and birk: moor and wood. *aislar:* ashlar.
orra sark: common shirt. *forfairn:* forlorn. *weirdless:* ill-fated.
tine the tid: lose the chance.

LOOKING SOUTH TO THE WALL

Here was the limit of empire, these fallen stones
the marchers raised on this bleak rolling land.
Lofty patricians, sick with their lust for Rome,
the brutal scarred centurions plumed and grand,
awaiting an easy action with defences planned,
bitterly holding a knuckle-end of dominion
to bolster a distant senator's good opinion.

Their eyes turned northwards to the restless clans
when in their own deep homeland the lesion lay
that turned to mockery their well-tested plans
and from this far limb drained the blood away.
This dead stone serpent marked their fleeting stay.
No wall, no ditch, no valorous legion's might
can hold the far frontier in time's despite.

JOHN ROY STUART

My face to the driving rain and my heart colder,
not in the fear of death, or exile from a mortal land;
fairer than this bleak moor the fields of France
where a smooth courtly language flows upon the tongue
in pleasant chateaux of the Loire.

Why should the heart yearn
for the drizzling crags of home and the poor hovels
that scatter the heather in the damp mists of the west:
a country of drovers, vendetta and harsh words,
of an old and dying poetry of forgotten heroes
and what in these brown glens or in all Scotland
could buy the elegance of one Parisian street?

Now that the walls of Dunedin of the Kings
no longer are defence, the only battlement
the hedge of my clenched teeth around a tongue
that carries the rough Gaelic of Strathspey.

This is the poor excuse, the last defence
that turns my face to the rain and breaks my heart.

I REMEMBER, I REMEMBER

The house where I was born, a ruin now.
Today I saw it after fifty years.
The window panes were shattered, beams brought low,
the rain running on stone like exile tears.
Strange that an image in the memory wear
a backlit glamour even into age
till truth writes colder history on the page.

Yet memory's bright lie was part of me:
those tumbled doors and walls and rotten stairs
were less a part of my reality
than the long dreaming; starkest ruin there
to stun the heart, to lay the ego bare
of false nostalgia laced like armour round
my dying body's muddy-mettled ground.

Poorly remembered house, shade of myself,
as much a ruin as I soon shall be.
Richer or poorer, sickness or in health
full circle brings a neater symmetry
between old age and youth's dead mystery.
The shivered glass, the moss, the fallen slate:
the misting mind beneath the balding pate.

MOORLAND PYLONS

High on the moorland the wind sings through wires
strung on the shoulders of the striding pylons.
What gods were robbed for these Promethean fires
in the tight prison on these iron columns?

Under the giants' feet bog-cotton grows;
sun's greater fire sinks to the distant hill.
Chained fire and free must to some junction flow,
pylon and stalk root in a common will.

SIMMER TIME

Simmer tid again an the whaups whustlan
in the gloamin licht upon the heich grunn,
an my een tak in the haill Wastlan
in the rid licht o the lang sun.

An auld man that sud ken better
nor staun here in a sheuch and gowp
et a wheen whaups an a sun settan.
Whitna thing tae gar the hert loup!

Simmer tid: Summer time. *whaup:* Curlew.
heich grunn ('ch' hard as in 'loch'): high ground. *Wastlan:* Westland.
een: eyes. *sud:* should. *nor:* than. *wheen:* few.
gar: compel. *loup:* leap.

THE HARNPAN
(Taen frae an auld Gaelic tale.)

Ae nicht as I wes waakin by the kirk
I spied an oabjeck liggin in the gress,
roon, white and glaizie lik a muckle baa.
Wi the heuk o ma stick I gied it a rare dunt
fur aa the warld lik drivan aff the tee.
It loupit twa-three yairds and gantit up,
an ugsome harnpan o some ither day.
Hou, said this ferlie wi a thrawnlik hoast
'd ye like yir ain heid skelpit wi a stick?
It seems a bodie canna lig in peace
and jouk the umrage of the leevin warld.

Ye maun forgie me, sir, I trummilt oot
it wisna my intent tae skite yir scaup;
forbye I didna ken et banes could speak.
I thocht the gabs of gaishens wad be steekit.
In onie case, gin I had ainlie kent
juist whit ye wir, the last thing I'd hae din
wad be tae yaise yir harnpan fur a die.
Is there onything, yir grace, that I micht dae
tae see ye yirdit fairly yince again?

—––>

Na, na, said he, *I've had eneuch o yon.....*
ma een and mooth and neb aa stown wi glaur.....
we naither braith nor sicht, lang days an dreich
nichts aye gae by withooten crack or claiver.
Nou, gin ye wad be quat of yon sair skelp
juist tak me hame and pit me on a stab
whaur a kin see and whiles hae a bit blether.....
and speak belike a ward whiles in yir lug
fur leevan chiels aye want for guid advice.

Weel, I gaed hame and pit him on a stang
atween twa busses on the gairden dyke.
Aa nicht he maun hae girnt and gantit there
ootbye amang the tattie-rigs and neaps,
but cam the morn the wife cam skreichan in.

Goad!   Whit's yon grugous scunner i the yaird?
Is yon a puggie's harnpan on the dyke?

Weel, I thocht, ye're the wumman that aye thinks
that ye ken mair nor onie ither sowl
but nou, belike, for yince I've bestit ye.
Yon, says I, *is a skelet that kin speak.*
Oot gaed I bauldly wi her et ma heels.

Heh, Maister Langsyne-Deid, says I
wull ye jist shaw this wumman ye kin taak?

—->

47

He keekit up wi yon fell sleekit smirk,
but not ae single cheep wad he lat oot
seean the wife luk dootsome doon her neb.
She didna say a ward but trintled aff.
Weel, ye'll jalouse, I felt a glaikit gowk.
Whit wey, I said, soorfaced, *did ye no speak?*

Ma wards, says he, *are ainlie fur yirsel.*
Aye syne yon scud ye gied me on the heid
we hae a kin o sibness you and me
we canna hae with onie ither bodie.
I taen the strunts and didna speak nae mair.

Weel, frae yon day, things gaed frae bad tae warse.
I wes no weel and bidit ben the hoose.
Last nicht the doacter whuspert in her lug
in yon douce-drumlie wey the craiters hae
when ye're ayont the pooer o their feesick.
An then, forbye she caat the laayer in
smilan and skailan oot a shaif o blauds,
stechan a pen intil ma wearie nieve.

Yon skelets herrit me o hale and siller;
Whiles nou she sets him on the chimla-brace
near whaur I yaised tae set.
Syne ilka fornicht whan the hoose is quait
I hear him whusper in his sleekit wey
the while she lauchs and skreichs lik onie wutch.
Gin ma waik shanks wad cairt me doon the stair
I'd dird him neb-doon in the kirkyard glaur.

—->

There's sticks fur kennlan and there's sticks fur gowf,
and here's some guid advice, gin ye'll tak tent:
yaise ilka gibble juist fur whit it's meant.

harnpan: a skull. *liggin:* lying. *glaizie:* shiny. *gantit:* stared.
ugsome: disgusting. *thrawnlike:* surly. *skelpit:* smacked.
umrage: spite. *scaup:* scalp. *gabs:* maws.
gaishens: skeletons. *steekit:* stitched. *yirdit:* buried.
dreich: dreary. *stab:* post. *busses:* bushes. *neaps:* turnips.
skreichan: yelling. *grugous:* horrid. *puggie:* monkey.
sleekit: sly. *neb:* nose. *trintled:* tripped. *jalouse:* surmise.
glaikit gowk: silly cuckoo. *scud:* a clout.
taen the strunts: took the huff. *douce-drumlie:* calmly serious.
shaif o blauds: sheaf of papers. *nieve:* fist. *herrit:* robbed.
chimla-brace: mantelpiece. *dird:* plant. *glaur:* mud.
kennlan: kindling. *gibble:* gadget.

MR BURNS FOR SUPPER.

Once a year, Robin, they will remember you
in a word or two beyond your actual name.
The fatuous speeches will scarcely encumber you,
the maudlin tear, the exaggerated claim.
Who love what you love measure your true fame
in a kind of silence the foolish find too great.
They take your measure by their own puffed state.

You who remembered Fergusson's smothered grave
when all but you had consigned him to oblivion;
placing his image in its proper frame
honoured the seed of your own inspiration:
the common urge to teach in song a nation
not merely sold but deliberately retarded
by those whose place enjoined on them to guard it.

In your occasional sploring they will seek
solace for their own indulgences to find,
but few enough of them will ever read,
that they may penetrate into the mind
hidden beneath that aching urge to rhyme
and scan in song this land's life and your own
wherein man is and will be made to mourn.

---->

The true admirer wonders how you did it.....
scribbling away in the midst of the Elect,
who seeing joy would hasten to forbid it,
suspicious of all but their own miserable respect
for a stone-age merciless god of their own construct
totally without love, an idol Christ did not know,
made from a kind of prurience welded into law.

Two worlds, the patient hoof and the ploughshare,
the high-fashion Dunedin drawing-rooms.
But you were happy neither here nor there.
The brief encounters of sex, the sabbath glooms,
whisky and hypocrites, the Presbytery of Ayr.
Coining your verses in the snirt and sneer
of peasant envy and the Yahweh-fear.

Still, you survived the capital's delights,
a Hesiod in the Athens of the North.
They came between your vision and the light:
a curiosity, not seeing your true worth
more than the western men of your own sort.
You found few listeners in either place:
the growing deafness of a sinking race.

Now, poets write books that Scotland does not buy,
shrink, in their eyes to the status of eccentric;
poetry's drowned out by every parrot-cry
feeding the multitude the latest cantrip.
They value verses less than a clownish trick;
once a year only within a phantom nation
they shrink your head to fit a social occasion.

IONA REMAINS (†)

In a crammed longship the ransackers came
to trample holy grass,
to stare without faith at saints,
to make a sacrifice of blood and fire.
Beloved island that lasts till the world ends.

In a crammed ferry new invaders come
to tread less heavily over the ancient paths;
to stare at old beliefs and turn away,
doubting their own doubt.
Beloved island that lasts till the world ends.

How pleasant it is to be upon an island
when the old terrors are forgotten;
where only the gulls scream now.

What plunder do they seek,
those city pilgrims walking with clouded eyes
among the crumbling tombs of warrior kings?
A chance to tread the machair once again,
to hear the same sea whisper,
to wrench the binding from the book of eternity.

A man of war became a man of peace,
stilled from the bloody, holy soil of Ireland.
Out from the abbey of the quiet wood
through Foyle's long water under beloved hills
to clasp far exile on an ancient rock.

(†) 'When the world comes to an   end, Iona will be as it was.'   Old Gaelic
poem.

—–>

How pleasant it is to walk upon an island
where fishers haul their nets to the sea's chant.

An island that lies still on the spirit's sea
clear when the days are clear;
lost when the high towers of the world
shadow the outline on the far horizon.

Blessed Icolmkill that stays till the world ends.
O holy island, rest again in our souls.

WILD GEESE

Saved from the North the geese
cry by the wintering loch,
fearless on our thin ice
in a sharp present that's undimmed by thought.

Their sight is not my seeing
by dark water and waving sedge;
closer to all true being
with their strong pinions beating the wind's edge.

WINTER WOODLAND

Lonely my walking in the woods;
slow is my step on fallen leaf,
flown from the tree the springtime brood,
the acorn in the earth asleep.

Until spring leaf the branch again
sun wake the seed from winter's death,
skies brighten after April rain,
lonely I walk the forest path.

OLYMPIAN DECISION

A caterpillar looped across the road,
by dire chance parted from his habitat,
with such a humble creeping motion that
I felt an urge to set up as a god,
ape the Far-Smiter, wield the lightning rod,
a hubris born of neither love nor hate.
I was the arbiter of his small fate:
whether to help him over, stamp him dead
or leave him as he was.   I let him go
to struggle onwards to the farther rim
and come by virtue to his motley wings.
Why I such mercy showed I do not know
when inner demons shouted: Flatten him!
Doubtless some hungry bird put paid to things.

THE UNKNOWN

When the unknown began to rattle and bang
immoderately in the empty room upstairs;
when, as if tipsy, it obscenely sang,
they blacked it out with everyday affairs.

The children, young, were balked by fairy tales.
Later, some explanation was required
for manic laughter and demonic wails
that kept them wide awake though overtired.

And, pat, when they divulged the family secret,
to their surprise it came as no surprise,
since the children said quite openly they knew it;
laughed at the guilt in their parents' turning eyes.

TIMON

After they've made it they become ungrateful.
Forget their pals now fallen on hard times.
Water in the face?   They asked for every plateful,
hoping for caviare and the best of wine.
Cold poverty's the medicine that refines
the fatty livers of the former rich
who ran their days on upper-crusty lines.
When the loot's gone and you're without a stitch.
they'll daub your reputation black as pitch.

It's a ball-breaking business.   I was a real swell,
ran my own horses, entertained the wits.
The uninvited found it sheerest hell
watching the smarter set who'd sit
guzzling and swilling and having a fabled fit
of laughter at *my* chat around *my* table.
No other place in town to equal it
for drink and wit and overpriced comestible.
Others had parties....Timon had a festival.

If I found gold buried beneath this pad
I couldn't care less, old boy, now that I've learned
it's only lolly, whether you have or had,
in the long run you'll only get your fingers burned.....
not that I've met the latest guru and turned.....
although it did rather come in a sudden flash
that flush or skint, you'll end up at the last
either by the in-crowd or pauper scribblers....spurned.

CUMHA BHALTAIR CINNEIDE (1450—1508?)

Chunnaic mi Bhaltair Cinneide
a' coiseachd troimh clach mo shul
fo sgail a' Chaisteal Dhuibh
aig am laighe na greine
is grinneal fo chois
air traigh liath Dhun Iubhair.

Ach cha robh e an leirsinn
duine air bith eile;
cha chuala iad a cheum
is cha b'urrainn dhaibh idir
a leabhar a leughadh
ged a shin e sin dhaibh;
chan fhaic a'ghraisg ud
an larach Ghillebhride
ach ballachan falamh
air am bu toigh leo
graffiti ur a sgrobail
anns a' chanain eile.

——>

IN MEMORY OF WALTER KENNEDY. *(Translation)*

I saw Walter Kennedy
walking through the apple of my eye
under the shadow of the Black Vault
at the time of sunset,
and gravel under his feet
on the grey beach of Dunure.

But he was not apparent
to any other person;
they did not hear his step
and they could not read his book
though he offered it to them;
that gang could see nothing
in Gilbert's ruin
but empty walls
where they were pleased
to scratch new graffiti
in another language.

SONG TO THE HIGHLAND DRESS

*(From the Gaelic of John MacCodrum c. 1748 after the banning of the
wearing of the tartan.)*

Sick and sore I am, worn and weary,
walking no more since my limbs are bound.
Cursed be the king who stretched our stockings
down in the dust may his face be found.
The length of our leg in these lubber wrinkles
scarce does such gear become a man:
better we loved our graceful short-hose
from heel to garter but a span.

Coats he'll allow us with tails a-flapping
shoes he'll leave us by the score,
but treat us with no trace of honour,
grabbing our gear to make us poor;
worse than all this he forces backsides
into these niggard peasant breeches,
knowing the spreading comely tartan‾
meant more to us than all our riches.

In this clumsy cassock I'm tangled nightly
can't stretch my legs, no wink of sleeping.
Better the ease of the ten yards single
that in the morning I'd be pleating —
a lightsome dress, kept wind and rain off
every gallant lad who had it:
the curse of the two worlds upon
the mean usurper who forbade it.

THE AULD GRUNN

They laucht whan I cam back tae the auld grunn;
watchan the dominie scart in the wersh yird,
heisan the slabs back on the cowped dykes,
makkin a bing o stanes ayont the heid-rigg.

They said: ye'll haurdly grow eneuch fir ane;
ye's get nae siller howkan yir guts oot there;
why sud a man o education try
tae wring his keep oot o yon histy grunn?

Settan lik lairds oan their fancy new machines,
mitherless dreggans breathan the reek o hell,
they keekt et me asklent, girnan tae ane anither
as if I'd taen ma lang daurg-days frae thaim.

But ma ain kin wrocht here, afore they left
the lane broon mosses fir the dowie touns:
this yird wes treisure tae me and its paibles gems,
thir drystane dykes ma castle's curtain wa.

Nou they play lounfu tricks when the daurk hides thaim,
they pit their bairns tae skreichan, cowp my dykes,
they thraw the seeds of dockens in ma corn.
But I hae stellt ma feet, and staun firm till I dee.

grunn: ground. *dominie:* schoolmaster. *howkan:* digging.
histy: barren. *daurg-days:* workdays. *wrocht:* worked.
mosses: moorlands. *yird:* earth. *lounfou:* lubberly.
stellt: braced.

——>

THE OLD CROFT
(Second Version: See 'The Auld Grunn')

They laughed when I came back to the old croft;
watching the dominie dig in the wersh ground,
heaving the slabs back on the cowped dykes,
making a bing of stone in the field corner.

They said: you'll only grow what feeds yourself;
there's little profit in howking your guts out there;
why should a man of education try
to wring his living out of yon histy park?

Sitting on top of their fancy new machines,
motherless dragons breathing the fumes of hell;
squinting at me, and girning to one another
as if I were stealing what I got from toil.

But my folk struggled here, before they left
the bare brown moorland for the choking towns.
This earth was treasure ground, its pebbles gems;
the grey stone dykes my castle's bastion.

Gaping through windows as I sit warm by the hearth
their mockery turns to envy and open spite;
desiring my peace but lacking my keen intent,
they have nothing left but what the strangers taught.

Now they play peasant tricks when darkness falls,
sending their lads to howl, cowping my dykes;
throwing the seeds of tares among my tilth.
But I have firmed my feet, and stay here till I die.

dominie: schoolmaster. *wersh:* sour. *cowp:* overturn.
bing: heap. *histy:* barren. *girning:* complaining.
park: field.

SIRENS

Grey Mr. Kroisos sit in the mezzanine,
watch the ghosts dancing on the dark sea;
salt in the eyes among cigars and wine
the tears flow back to childhood poverty.

Barelegged in the narrow harbour street,
hungry and supple, tuned by sirocco and sun.
Flesh now corruptly sated with all meats,
ashes and dust are the battles you have won.

Recall again the bloomed and swollen grapes
whose bursting juice fermented your warm youth;
call no man happy till the ultimate
vintage is pressed from the sharp fruits of truth.

——>

Now lost the raven's wing, bold flashing eye,
the first hot kiss of your dear native earth.
In your shrunk heart a zephyr of old sighs
breathes once again remembered peasant worth,

against the discords, fat on alimony,
deserted Circes of a passing spell
who roused at last no lust or charity.
Horns of today's dilemma fit you well

crossing slim legs to plan with slanted eyes
smiling denial of senile vigilance.
Lackeys provoke her list of memories
of brief delights sparked by such happy chance.

The white craft is becalmed in the blue bay.
No need to bid them bind you, stop your ears;
the songs they sing are faded quite away,
evade the summons of both wealth and tears.

EDDERS AND AIPPLES

Edder on the dyke-back
whitna gear is't ye lack?
Sempil Adam, warm Eve
yir slee cantrips tae prieve.

Wee reid aipple, whit sin
dernit deep in yir skin
drave wud oor first mither,
pit him in a swither?

Adam's sin, Eden's law
whitna maitter ava,
sairpent's trick, aipple's bree
tae an auld man lik me?

Edder: Adder. *Aipple:* Apple. *sempil:* simple.
cantrip: tricks. *prieve:* prove. *reid:* red *dernit:* hidden.
swither: quandary. *bree:* juice. *wud:* mad.

OLD SOLDIER

How could I know that after the bold campaigns
under the ablest commanders I'd come to this:
scrimping my last years out in a town's remains
under a slattern roof in a gap-walled place,
the chosen of neither one nor another race.
Find at the end of all that a promised prosperity
bleeds to a sorry shift at an empire's extremity.

Here, clowns wax proud of their right to be included
within their own sorry ploys that make do for truth;
regard for courage or brains that once was rooted
has gone from the marrow; now the easy and crude
gain all approval.   Whenever a plan is viewed
by the fishy eyes of dolts.....merit's a threat,
restraint the luxury of a time that's dead.

I have neither sword nor buckler nor promised ground.....
I have neither plate nor harness nor tossing plume;
no marching in triumph, no drum and no trumpet sound,
only grey stiffening limbs in a ramshackle room
where there's little else to do but mutter and fume
while the youngsters mock me with their seeming sooth:
all men, old man, were heroes in their youth.

VISION

Personal devils spring from too much drink;
madonnas show to an obsessive piety.
The world from such extended viewpoint shrinks,
frames sense to a neat pentagon sobriety.

The tune is kindled in one variant soul
though many chanting choirs may share the song.
When vision's tethered to a common role
extend a side to prove a theorem wrong.

POSTHUMOUS FAME

Do poets now at rest in their new mansions
look through the windows of eternity
to view from these Parnassian expansions
their work examined by posterity?

Ah, hear them say, that's not the thing at all
I meant to say the day I wrote the song,
but what I meant to say I can't recall
and even if I could, they'd get it wrong.

RELIGIOUS INSTRUCTION

On Monday morning he is required to give
Religious Instruction since the law demands it.
Whether or not it affects the way they live
his obligation's plain, and so he hands it
to their adolescent minds like a weekly ration:
the proofs of God's existence in teacher fashion.

Trying to be even-handed.   Protestant as Knox
he coaxes belief in them like any Jesuit.
The wide-bottomed boat of Western smugness rocks;
jetsams the rules with which they ballast it.
If another hidden kingdom gleams behind
their Monday morning eyes, it does not shine.

Religious Education must be contained
in their first forty minutes; there are more
significant mysteries to be explained.
Physics and Chemistry will soon restore
any small leak that holiness may make.
Only radiation can burn us at the stake.

WORLDLY AIMS

As a mad ant may push a sawdust grain
thinking he has a wheat-ear in his claw,
by the vain summit of my years, again,
plans for new hopeful enterprise I draw.
That which I seek I know may not be given:
succeeding, further seeking is my care.
Suspended then, beneath this idiot's heaven
the hard ground rushes up as I tread air.
Yet if in vacancy I pass the day
I am mere ox that waits the killing-shot.
Rhymers must rhyme again as priests must pray.

Dumb poets, prayer-dry priests, are surely caught
within the nexus of the common beast
that lives in both.   The sawdust grain is best.

SPRING DROWNING

Plunging from the overhanging bough,
the few late seconds of a stripling life
led swiftly to the final knowledge: now.....
the cold wounded his body like a knife.

Joying in spring he would not think to go
to sudden darkness as the mirror broke
and loosed him to the winter mountain's snow
that lay in wait beneath the cloven rock.

The thrill of death thrusting through the ribs' cage
to set him gasping in the drumming dark;
to leave them mourning in a grievous rage
the callous smooring of his brief bright spark.

SEPTEMBER SHEAVES

Now I have lost a joy that pleased my soul,
looking from this window up to the long park,
where now the giant combine grunts and rolls
to get the lot done between dawn and dark.

I mind the day when on this sloping face
the golden sheaves stood like a waiting host
stook upon stook; today with little grace
their haste will swallow what my eye loved most.

SHEEP

Sociably munching, a bachelors' club of rams
carry their *raison d'etre* between their hams.

Soon they will be divided by their duty:
transmitting the blood-line of ovine beauty

to the next cavorting troop of silly lambs
growing to the seeming end of ewes and rams.

An unvicious circle which seems to have one point:
supplying mankind with a jersey and Sunday joint.

MORNING FROST

Threescore years now and bare trees again,
a crisp morning frost as white's my beard.
I still shout vainly to the world of men:
Listen, listen, for I will be heard.

They will as resolutely turn their backs
as old men did on me when I was young:
they will hear nothing of mere dreams or plain fact,
set me to doubt myself when all is done.

Empty the mind, the only thing that's left,
for there's no cure for them if they won't see.
When of this last foul itch I am quite bereft
remains whiteness of frost, bare blackness of tree.

SOCIAL CHANGE

Fallen stones in the clearing of the wood.
I can recall when walls rose proud and high
to house an even prouder family.
There's nothing lives here but the weasel's brood.

How sure they were: that grave patrician dame;
the tall, calm gentleman who ruled this place.
Now memory's error shadows their sure grace,
dulls the fine echo of an ancient name.

But why should I regret, whom they ignored?
Their passing surely matters none to me.
A trifling service I performed for fee:
tumbling these walls; burning each rotten board.

POWER

These sleeping stones are yet
filled with all power:
all between birth and death
sleeps in this flower.

Which in quiet beasts that graze
looks to my passing.
In my own being prays
power everlasting.

MAY DAY

Suddenly the rain's gone and the grey veil clears.
Bleak winter's threat warms from our sight away.
Plumbed is the void of our cold northern fears
as grudging April swells to welcome May.
Green through red earth the harvest-promise shows,
green slopes the valley to the distant blue
of far-off hills; now all the rich earth knows
that leaf and life return, all's made anew;
the scene that was and will be and holds yet
the linking essence of the wasted past,
the rotted leaf and the long-broken frame.
Under this sun's bright embrace all regret
must vanish now, and vanish in our last
long winter to a vaster spring again.

MAN WALKING

On the hill-slope man merges into trees,
loses particular, melts to stone and grass
where following breezes lend him a swift ease
as he strides on past all so all things pass;
all blood and sap beats warmly through one heart,
all sight is gathered to the falling sun;
no leg or stalk or trunk that moves apart,
the sinews of all being move as one.
The vein runs crystal, blood flows in the stream,
blossom on flesh and bush, sky set in gold,
eye that sleeps sound within a waking dream.
True power all motion in his cupped hands hold
in a warm grasp that merges heart and mind,
all separateness turned to a common kind.

KIERKEGAARD

Breeches, however warm, if incomplete
focus the interest of the sniggering plebs.
Dreaming regardless in the city street
the sage wore trousers with uneven legs.

Profanum vulgus simply doesn't care
for the well-tailored thoughts within the head.
Odd trouser legs are much more its affair;
eggheads occasion mirth until they're dead.

SPIDER STORY

Swing spider.   So I concentrate my mind.

Food after battle, licking bloody hands.
The southern voice: you eat your countrymen.
Those I had slain shrugged off for rebel bands
fittingly dead for their foul plundering.
Now they seem close to me as my blood kin
who saw as virtue what I took for sin.

In holy sanctuary I sought quiet talk,
cool words to mellow a hot difference.
I could not guess that flaring pride would balk,
swift point stab out to where I saw offence.
A single sacrilegious death unplanned
bids me slay many in the Holy Land.

What wars are evil and what battles just
priests of all armies eagerly debate.
I, who lie cold here, fight because I must.
Vassal repentance has been left too late.
I fight for life and land and if I fall
plead cause alone to the liege-lord of all.

Swing spider.   So I concentrate my mind.

LARK

Lark sings as she has always done
over the thorn hedge of the spring meadow.
Now my time's very nearly run.....
long gone the day of the coarse fellow
who heard the song and indifferently whistled
and thought of beef and beer and fun and girls,
ignoring warnings of his careless heading.

Now Lark has a deal more of attention;
a careful leaning on the broken gate.
I think of the subject we try not to mention,
former abstractions of our certain fate,
cold speculations on threescore and ten.
Sing Lark, sing Lark to me and then
perhaps the scented hour will seem less late.

DISTANCE

Ignorantly going where the path goes,
my feet on earth, the coldest wind on cheek,
I see on far hilltops remaining snows,
losing in distance what I mainly seek.

The landscape's mystery is no great matter,
where logic stumbles over its own rule.
From layered sky down to the great water
reflection breaks upon a rippling pool.

A KNELL FOR MR. BURNS

I think of you Mr. Burns
lying in your death bed;
sweating and sick by turns,
desperate dreams in your head.

In articulo mortis beset
lacking a tailor's fee:
seven guineas in debt
for a worldly vanity.

A day or so after you'd gone
wherever poets go,
the great world looked upon
your fate with affected woe.

Played the Dead March in Saul
behind your silent remains,
having valued hardly at all
the moving heart and brains.

Strange that the living face
should suffer so much rage,
while birth-and-burial place
grew to a pilgrimage.

LANDSCAPES

Young, I recall standing on a fair shore,
my gaze fixed on an island whose soaring peaks
called to me: *come, this is the place of the heart.*
The more I turned the eye would turn the more,
the more I looked aside the more the eye would seek
the secret land that won my whole regard.
I know that island now as well as I know my hand;
its shores are no more to me than my home tides.
I see other hills that I have much desired
become the mere hill-slopes of a known land.
The distant horizons that blazed in the eager mind
shrink to familiar lanes of a quiet shire.

Now I look on these known hills
knowing: this is not home, but away, away
over the green landscapes the heart pursues eternity
and is never satisfied, never filled.
But after all gazing there will come a day
when all landscapes will solace the heart's infinity.

YELLOW CHARLIE GUNN

Strong drink and bad light
made yellow his face;
tholing fools for a bite,
giving songs for a grace.

Holes in his britches,
holes in his shoes;
sleeping in ditches
gave him the screws.

Think of the times,
forget all the rest,
when he made the sweet rhymes
that would tighten the chest.

HOMEWARD

There is no hope of breaking through this cloud
or dragging comfort from this speaking wind;
these are the cold companions of my stride
over low moorland where no mark is found.

Let all worn words and faded reasons shrink,
patter of priests and the confessors sigh.
Follow the grey rough road and do not think,
window the landscape through a steady eye.

Stretch step to be rid of these dull elements,
to cloister tedium in familiar walls;
come to known hearth from gloomy firmament,
to loved, small flame before the darkness falls.

EVOLUTION

Nature perhaps has finished with us now;
her favoured selection ends in a blast of fire
having withdrawn too far from the scythe and plough,
winter's cold furrow and the spring's desire.
Hemmed within tall streets she will burn us down
vainglorious, that such exit was our choice
who had stolen her power for our orb and crown;
by this our planned petard most grandly hoist.
But that which we call nature or other thing
may have seen no usefulness in our gross pride
that rules the fathoms, outsoars the eagle's wing
and thrusts all peace and sanity aside.

Yet singed like moths in evolution's flame
the undying ghost may seek some other frame.

ERNCROGO
(Crogo's place.)

The grandson of the winged helmet
who gave this croft its name
burned the blood from his steel
and burnished it in this sour earth
behind a sweating ox.
The centuries have shared him out
among the sullen vanquished:
his eyes, his hair, his stride
adorn the walkers on the moorland path
who pass with peaceful greeting.

A shepherd gazes
over a drystone dyke
leaning on his crook as on a spear.
Calmly through his blue stare
old Crogo muses on the silent land.

THE DEATH OF THE
TECHNICAL MISSIONARY

He wanders lost, a body without blood,
undone by Prester John's unseemly magic.
He, in his mortal flesh yearned for their good;
they unregenerate, did not see as tragic,
lack of transistors, cathode, anode, grid,
but with their knobkerries crushed in his head.

Bone-shattered by that wizard's evil planning,
stronger than chant, more powerful than sign,
he tried to preach to backwoods understanding
a vision of the Piccadilly Line.
I've heard, said John, *these subterranean bores*
end in a market-place for drugs and whores.

Blood of dark slaughter in the thirsty earth,
his skeleton dispersed to no avail,
whose cerebration might have given birth
to World Broadcasts of their tribal tales.
The end of silicon and chips, John said:
diluting truth to fit the thickest head.

He haunts the trees, from every organ severed
while John keeps things the way they used to be.
Surgical miracles he'd have uncovered,
replacing their worn organs frequently.
Cover your ears, John told his simple clods,
a man dies when his time's up with the gods.

DANTE

Saddened by passion, cruelly sick from war
he held the eternal in a writing hand;
trusting a lodestone pen that steered him far
into those bounds wherein all men must stand.
Now, hubris, masked to make a better case
strings out transcendence on a counting-frame
to shrink creation in an easier name.
Finding that mere contrivance lacks a soul,
no new addition to the Florentine;
they seek, to wrap up conscience from the cold,
mankind in their mechanics to confine.

But their flawed blueprint does not change the state
of charted coastlines where three kingdoms wait.

CONVERT

On his way northwards on business from the city
his mind, they say, suddenly became affected
in a way not totally unconnected
with a sneaking spark of unconventional pity
engendered by watching once a steadfast heretic
paying the ultimate price for his trendy views
about life, death, after-death and alleged good news.
The stubborn determination of this fanatic
seems to have been reflected in the watcher's mind
so that he began to shudder and hear voices,
develop a nervous defect of the sight.
Thenceforth from respectability he wholly declined
to a low way of life marked by absurd choices
and soap-box proclamations of seeing the light.

BLITHE SPIRIT

In spring's first glow these heroes were sounding forth,
filling the air with their bright joyous sound.
Unkindly for us all in such a month
the crisp snow smothered all our growing ground.

Cheerless, we glared from windows as the cold
nipped the new blossom, chilled the shooting earth,
laid on all life its frosty five-day hold,
kept the hill-walker reading by the hearth,

till going out to fetch a pail of coal
when even our warmed roofs were still unthawed
I heard again the clear, bright, singing call.
In the chill azure a brief summer glowed.

AUTUMN LIGHT

In the slant light of the autumn afternoon
the little waves run gold up to the cladach.
Again it is granted to be here alone
after the dull days, the long dry plodding.

The wind sighing down red and saffron leaves
across the stippled gold and green of the moor.
These sights and sounds I am given should bring all ease,
yet I do not find that which I came here for.

Though distance and peace here are in good supply
for any man of sense who could use them aright
I see but dimly with that inner eye,
must be content with this more worldly light.

BARDS

Some talk of Alexander, and some of Hercules,
but for some dusty rhymester, who would have heard of these?

The limner, the piper and the bard
are your only true aristocrats.
For all his battle-thumpings and tent-snivellings
Achilles owes everything to the poet.
The adulterous and mendacious Ulysses
would have added a mere pinch to Ithacan dust
had his deeds not been strung between the horns of a lyre.

Our fathers knew if they wanted a wartless picture
the limner had to be housed, the piper paid.
The bard, most dangerous of the three,
must be pampered, petted *and* paid
to stave off a skin-ripping satire that made your friends
point fingers at you and laugh out loud
until the whole of your body burst into boils.

A bard who was given a cow when he wanted a horse
once squared the reckoning with a wicked rhyme.
Better pay up, avoid a grandchild's curse.

---->

Now no one listens to bards; they do not make good telly.
But think, when they dig up the shards of our broken times,
cathode ray tubes will be smashed, oxides destroyed,
but a piece of quality foolscap may survive
with your name on it.

Just like that other plutocrat
whose churlish habit it was
to give cows instead of horses.

ARCHILOCHUS

Earning your spear-bread in a hard-voiced camp
dodging the column of the well-bred fool,
your soldier's eye preferred the bow-legged scamp
with battle tactics under his red wool.

Losing poems in the heat of bloody slaughter,
lying between campaigns in a bored black rage,
having lost that anxious daddy's precious daughter,
(too well brought up to wed with a half-slave).

Abandoned shields, foppish or ginger leaders,
overfond fathers guarding their ewe-lambs.
In your iambics these are much better treated
than you by refused kinship or battle-plans.

DISPOSSESSED POET (‡)

Poor Davie Broderick grew sour
to see the gentry come to naught.
Tight-counted syllables of power,
the measures that the schools had taught,

a mystery to boor and fool.
The simpler measures are their meat:
hucksters can't bear the classic rule,
prefer the rhythms of the street.

Poor Davie starved and tramped the road
counting the feet within his head,
such poet tricks his only load,
his wish but to be swiftly dead.

For death he thought a better state
than turning penny-tavern-rime.
When parvenus replace the great,
Old bards must bow to fickle time.

(‡) *Daibhidh O Bruadair, bard to the Fitzgeralds.*

I INTENDED A SONNET

Petrarch set out a scheme for warmer climes
than this chill North, wherein a formal mind
struggles for a whole fourteen lines to bind
true verse without resort to mere half-rhymes;
a knotty task which all bards think at times
impossible; Italians could easily find
lexical items of a matching kind
just like a set of *campanello* chimes.
Tempi, avanza, empi and *speranza*
flooded the *lessico* of Frankie Petrarca;
even minor poets can rattle off a stanza
with fifty thousand choices of end-marker.
Bending the word-hoard to an Italian sonnet
made even honest Will cry: out upon it!

ILIAD

The heroic society follows me on the road
as I attend once more the rites of Patroklos,
feeling, even at this distance, a shared loss.
Far over the plain I see bronze harness glow
across the dead ground of shrouding centuries
wherein the pattern of our latter day was sown;
shouts echo though the tracks are overgrown.
Throughout all time the seeded warriors rise
upon the blooded earth to fight again;
swift through steel air above another plain
mighty and further-striking javelins fly
their fated missions in an Olympian sky.
No bright hexameters confine our rage
but slaughters headlined on an indifferent page.

INQUE BREVI SPATIO MUTANTUR

The bells ring from the square tower change upon change
loud in the green mowing meadows of high summer.
Held in their music lovers walk with love
closer to birth than sudden and whispering death.
Flat water and whispering trees and cotton cloud,
youth burning in flesh like fire, unquenchable fire.

Trusting that time will never cool their fire,
caught by the changing bells in a time without change.
Only the flint tower has seen enough of summer
and of all lovers walking sweet with love.
The marriage binding, the blessing of babes and death
pass under the arch and are darkened as by a cloud.

A wayless wandering under sun and cloud;
the wasting of winter tempers the summer's fire.
Hand parts from hand as the glowing lovers change,
sadden as the light pales in their late summer,
yearning for the lost warmth of all past love
they shrink from the amorous overtures of death.

Yet all shall couple in the marriage-bed of death;
the warm sky of youth his sure, cold breath shall cloud
to hope of heaven or terror of hell-fire:
chime after chime the bell rings to that last change
till young hearts and old bones both shall be warmed by
                                                      summer
bending to the rich choice of a greater love.

--->

And death's cold kiss shall be thawed by a later love;
neither lasting of this life nor dominion of death,
but a brightness of brightness shall burn away the cloud
with a mighty love that burns beyond passion's fire,
beyond flesh, beyond bone and grave and our time's
change
in the joyful meadows of eternal summer.

Walk then, young lovers in the happy fields of summer
knowing the greater love that lies beyond your love.
Thinking on life be not unmindful of death.
All one are bells and whispering trees and cloud.
Beyond all earth and air and water and fire
the unchanging waits for all, eternal in our change.

MODERN BIOGRAPHY

The fashion now is not to admire the head;
that will have had its share of adulation.
Our gaze moves down below the waist instead
to put the egregious in their proper station.
No matter what bright impulse, what new skill
forced head and shoulders out above the crowd,
be sure a time of subfusc scraping will
uncover something that's not quite allowed:
some curious coupling, something done in dark,
small peculations, meanness in the rich.
Such tales on stilts soon quench the eternal spark;
the shine of gold is soon drowned under pitch.

Throw mud at saints to balance out the odds,
great men *sans* flaws would not be great, but gods.

NICHOLAS HERMAN (‡)

No frame he found to combat telescopes
but his dark winter tree: bare, grim and high,
a leafless gallows on the fading sky,
more to his mind deep that a thousand tropes
of the dry schoolmen, tight in their close groups
wrangling the wherefore and the doubtful why
that gives no answer to the common cry
that mankind's ills be balanced by their hopes.

Despite bleak winter and the inner dark,
bare trees will bud, and branch its flower bear,
bright summer call spring's burgeon into leaf;
beyond all discourse, this the promised mark.
To minds untrammelled by the scholar's care
all answer lies between the seed and sheaf.

(‡) *Brother Lawrence, the 'Kitchen Saint'.*

NON-ACADEMIC GROUP

Weigh up the talents of the Bronze Class:
Without grace they await the day of freedom,
the light armed warriors who shall not pass
but do not look in any way defeated.

Ignorant of aorist, quadratic, participle,
they view with tolerance the polymath,
knowing in their red hearts: we are the people,
our hewing and drawing is the nation's breath.

Happily released, legs braced firmly upon planks,
muscularly moving concrete, bricks and steel,
they wave in mockery to the Golden ranks
who, struck by madness, chose to stay in school.

Their point is made: Euclid, however smart,
never raised up a solid Perpendicular.
In the hammer and shovel day of their strong art
Bronze is the general stay of Gold's particular.

THE PLACE FOR POETRY

Sundry poets cultivate
a locative abandon:
Auden hotfoots to the States
Eliot to London.

Virgin muses hope to find
lurking among strange races;
poetry's pinpoint is the mind.
little to do with places.

Parnassus, Athens, Inverness,
Tintern or Timbuktu,
setting a scan to inwardness
any old place will do.

SCAPEGOAT

When he had stowed the powder in the can,
rammed home the nails like peas within a pod,
he watched his day's work tear apart a man,
strolled home and wrote a poem, blaming God.

RURAL BARD

Who strolls in the rumbling city
courting the urban Muse
must show himself to be witty,
brace up his soul with booze.

Bore on poetical fringes,
his maggot hole in The Few;
for he knows he won't be printed
till the Big Boys nod him through.

But here in the spuds and pumpkins
may write whatever he will;
the Laureate of the Bumpkins
in Parnassus-under-the-Hill.

Envoi:

Squire,
Country poets are not much read
though locally well-known;
even the poacher taps his head
and points to the poet's home.

POETRY LESSON

What's poetry?
Much easier, sir, to say what it is not.
Somewhere between the words the poetry's caught.
To put it another way: the bit that's fated
to disappear whenever it's translated.

The best words in the best order?
Agreed.   But don't use rhymes except the ones like 'murder'.
and not too much regular iambic scansion,
it leads, you'll find, to much too much expansion.

Sorry.
That's it, you've got it then,
just a man speaking to plain men.

If it doesn't rhyme or keep time?
Never mind.   Write it like prose
chopped up into rows
making sure no one knows
or can find out
what exactly you're talking about.
Before long you'll be highly Prized
and much anthologised.

104

SCARECROW

Mark well this dummy with the grinning face
who cannot know his head is stuffed with straw,
a ragged ruffian tailored to his place
as watchman of the seed that others sow.
His flapping rags that were broad cloth and fine
to suit a soul whose blood ran warm with love
on this crow-starving sentry end their time
round jackstraw limbs whose sinews cannot move.
Fair flesh has yielded to his wooden frame
no image dances in his vacant eye,
dawnlight and midnight dark are all the same,
he's lodged in earth until his time's gone by.
Those tatters held a finer form within
that in its turn became this scarecrow's twin.

SHRINK
See Inferno: XX: 11—16

Professional charmer.....circulates in heads
the claim to rid the world of god and devil.
He conjures up from childhood garden sheds
dark ghosts to quit us of our present evil.

Heir to the spells of all past wizardry.
The ancient jargon's quite transmogrified.
Rise from his psychomantic couch and see
his head still turned towards his own backside.

TEACHER

He marked them present, absent, churned them out:
subtractors, adders, some could even read.
Society's future crops he sowed about
but got no credit for the growing seed.

Year after year the generations flew
under his eye; some even heard him speak.
All parted gladly.   What he thought they knew
most of them shed when they'd been gone a week.

UNPUBLISHED POETS

See there the proud ones of the bardic school
draw their cloaks round them as they make their way
to the great hall through gawping knave and fool
and some who tailor verse as well as they.

They look with angry spite on those who sing
songs to the lesser folk with the same art
that they by merest perseverance bring
to long fruition.   We speak from the heart

but still count syllables to suit the mood
of joy or sadness, loneliness or love
that touch us too; although of meaner blood
these in our humbler veins as surely move.

No gifts of gold or horses do we take
who do but make the song for the making's sake.

INDE CADUNT MORTES

As usual there is a proliferation of dead things
flattened or broken up on the hill road
at intervals marked out by the ravens' wings
having been twined from life by some speeding Toad.
One might think, this is a nice balance when
our human progress provides a corbie's dinner
while giving a strange divinity to men
for a fell instant be they saint or sinner,
on the sole criterion of mindless speed
that lends no time for sentiment or brake.
While rabbits, like their betters, take no heed
but risk swift death for a mere whimsy's sake.
Mankind to mankind less indifference shows:
we kill for spite as well as feeding crows.

HISTORY LESSON

A king, to solve their politics and his,
set rival gangs to fighting on the Inch:
the Cat-men and the Kays.   They clanged and battered,
spoiled the axe-edges, locked the Islay hilts.

The Cat-men hired a bandy-legged smith
who lopped the heads off all Clan Kay but one.
He poured his blood into the Tay's cool water
swimming from a Scotland he could not understand
back to an Alba that was yet familiar.

It still goes on.   Lolling on benches
well railed off from the clans, our rulers watch.
There is no river we can dive into.

ART AND SALVATION

The meenister o Heich Drumclairtie
(mock-Tudor villas, chromium pub
whaur big-wamed baillies hale an hearty
discuss the local yachting club).....
he's no content tae ding doun sinners
in dowie sermons i the kirk.....
maun pit puir scrievers aff their dinners
and dae a poetry critic's work.

The meenister of Heich Drumclairtie
is no content wi chasin Clootie;
ilk upstert rhymester, ilka bardie
maun thole the tae o's godlie bootie.....
and when he's no at sic derision
maks crambo-clinkers boke and chitter
he gies wee chats on television
tae make thaim for salvation fitter.

The meenister o Heich Drumclairtie
expert on verse baith rhymed an free
scrieves columns fur a union pairtie
and kens a iamb frae a spondee.
Baith verse an sin he judges rarely;
atween the Muses an Salvation
he seeks tae strike a balance fairly....
a ane-man telly-kirk sensation.

--->

The meenister o Heich Drumclairtie
loups twixt the halo an the bays,
swithers frae godlie warks tae arty
an in baith warlds demands a say.
The bardic and the kirklie caa
share equal pairts in his vocation.....
pray then that he may never faa
atween thaim baith tae his damnation.

scriever: writer. *Clootie:* the Devil. *crambo-clinker:* rhymer.
boke an chitter: gag and shiver. *swither:* hesitate.

ENVOI TO THE DEAN'S BOOK

He was concerned greatly for old forms,
even those of swaggering and predatory bards.
Three hundred pages (octavo in gilded boards)
of ill-spelt Gaelic that sought therein to catch
the spirit of a passing time; to clutch
anxiously under dead, decorated wings
the still strong mustiness of ancient things.

My own edition, more the worse for wear
than any vellum; full of scholar's notes,
comparisons of varying recensions where
what the bards say may seem of less import
than learned surmise is, however short.
Vauntings, laments and measured homiletics
now share the page with variant phonetics.

A Gaelic link that is not mere sentiment
(tourist guide-book, spoken on holiday
to the MacBrayne's steward, Clan society merriment
or brief patriotic toasts for Saint Andrew's Day)
gets to the heart of Scotland in the keenest way.
The black jewel of Aiffric's grief set against gold
remains until this hour as bright and cold.

—->

Fearful between two ages the good Dean tried
to squeeze the best he knew into small case.
But for his pains Red Finlay would have died,
the bard MacLintock would have ceased to chase
profit by toadying to Duncan's race
in the best *Ae Freislighe* he could summon forth,
hoping, no doubt, to win himself a horse.

But Scotland remains indifferent to such work,
save for a few eccentrics like myself,
madmen, in the great world's view, who lurk
under the shadow of a dusty shelf,
where at the far and least illuminated edge
all that is truly Scottish is confined
far from what passes as the native mind.

FAUR AHINT MAUN FOLLOW FASTER (‡)

I hae follow't ye aboot, Maister Burns
frae the Auld Toun o yir birth
thro Dunedin o the Kings
tae the Doonhamer-land o yir daith
whase mool I micht weel share.

Aa the years o my bairntid yir face lukt doon,
as I snoovilt by the Square on the wey tae schuil,
the Clydesdales cletterin on the causey-stanes,
herds aff the Burns Laird boat swirin et dugs and stots
caa'in thaim on tae the mercat o Tam's mishanter.

I kent the bien wee biggin o yir birth
gey near as weel's ma ain;
I ken the braw twa-laftit hoose ye dee't in.....
skinnt, o coorse.....
but sodgers,burgesses, baunds blawin up the Deid March,
they gied ye a graund send-aff.

Then there wes Edimbro fir the pair o us.....
whaur just the howffs tak muckle tent o makkars.....
tho mair fir bardic drouth than Muses' sough.

‡ *The title is a Scottish proverb meaning that those left behind must make*
stouter efforts.

——>

An nou I'm cam tae whit ye never wir.....
an auld soor bodach wi a lyart baird,
staunin ablo the statue the Doonhamers biggit.
The caurs birl roon aboot, the horse hae gane
binnae ahint the Cornet yince a year.
Wha is't that kens ye wadna gie a snirt
tae see ye stell't atween a feenancial hoose
and the vauntie steeple o Calvin's muckle kirk?

I share an thole the same byornar stangs
in this auld land o deean herts and leids
whaur the paircel o rogues hes swallt tae a haill bing;
I'm kittled by yon maist unwycelike yeuk
fir scrievin in the 'aulder Scottish tongue'.....
a thenkless daurg I'm shair ye maun agree.

Roon auld St. Michael's just the ither day
I daunnert by thon dowie scartit stanes
lik gable-ens of hooses haudin doon
(anent a resurrection faur owre shin)
the banes o lairds and laayers, dochtless nou.

I cam fornenst yon unco mausoleum
they biggit owre ye et the hinner en
howkin yir banes up eftir twintie year
in sempler yird; last lap o towrist pilgrimage
roon Grecian temple, ferms and stanes and banes
that mark yir pheesical curriculum vitae
athoot being owre fasht by yir leevin spirit.

——>

But I'll no girn, Maister Burns, fir eftir a
et least they gied ye twa-three momuments.....
an haud a kin o saunt's day yince a year.....
brak haggis thegither an share a sacred tassie
of coansecraitit yill or usquebae.
Man..... yon's a puckle mair than they hae duin
fir Scotland's twintie score negleckit bards.

Even gin the feck o yir yince a year admirers.....
dinna seem tae me, on the evidence
tae ken whit 'twes ye wir ettlin tae say.

The Auld Toun: Ayr.   *Doonhamer-land:* Dumfries.
mool: clay.   *bairntid:* Childhood.   *snoovilt:* slunk.
causey-stanes: cobbles.   *stots:* bullocks.   *mercat:* market.
mishanter: mishap.   *bien wee biggin:* cosy little house.
twa-laftit: two-storied.   *howffs:* pubs.   *makkars:* poets.
drouth: thirst.   *sough:* whisper.   *bodach:* old man.   *lyart:* grey.
binnae: except for.   *snirt:* snigger.   *vauntie:* proud.
muckle kirk: big church.   *thole:* endure.
byornar stangs: uncommon stings   *leids:* languages.
haill bing: whole heap.   *kittled:* tickled.   *unwycelike yeuk:* foolish
itch.   *scrievin:* writing.   *daurg:* labour.   *shair:* sure.
maun: must.   *daunnert:* strolled.   *dowie:* gloomy.
scartit: scratched, carved.   *faur owre shin:* far too soon.
dochtless: powerless.   *forenenst:* opposite.   *unco:* amazing.
biggit: built.   *hinner en:* latter end.   *howkin:* digging.
sempler yird: simpler earth.   *girn:* complain.   *tassie:* cup.
yill: ale.   *usquebae:* whisky.   *puckle:* little.   *feck:* majority.
ettlin: trying.

EXILE

Now all the blood that soaked the heather roots
has dried.   The old bards lie forgotten.
Given this new complaisance, these tame towns,
changing my favour I might yet return
to the long strath of flowing memory,
to summer trickle and to winter flood,
contained once more within the loving tribe.

Yet, when all goes,in exile there is honour.
Although I stumble in an alien tongue,
I am not shamed to smothering my own.
These foreign hills may be dressed well enough
to friendlier seeming by the inner eye.

Sometimes a comrade in this banishment
passes a greeting in our old lost speech.
The blood races; the heart lifts up in hope.
Though there is talk between us of returning,
behind the handclasp and the eye's bold eagerness
we know our old ways fail in the far country.

See, from the window, these mountains that top our own,
their valleys riper than our rocky glens.

Why should heart sadden for the native hills?

VIEWPOINT: LAMBDOUGHTY

On the far side of Straiton, on the hill road
the farm names change to Gaelic.
So does the country, bare moorland with no fences,
the rock teeth tearing at the base of clouds.
Look over the covenanting monuments
desperately stabbing the heavens;
you will see beyond the spent volcano of Creag Ealasaid
the distant bounds of the Lordship:
Arran, Kintyre and Jura.

The broken promises of history
are drowned within the silence.

FINDABAR'S SONG

Beside the pool still grows the rowan tree
whose blooded branches shade the monstrous deep;
in all my hours of waking day or sleep
he brings a red branch to the shore for me.

No memory of love remains but this;
white skin, black hair, clear eyes and death's dark flood
scarlet of spilling berries and of blood
to me more dear than his forgotten kiss.

DONEC REQUIESCAT

False memory feels the mud between the toes,
builds moated castles by the warm sea's edge,
recalls a bank whereon the wild thyme grows,
scents love-time roses in a summer hedge.

Tomorrow's breeze may speed the vessel home
blown by long sighs from the vain land of hope:
come, cakes and ale and gold and shining stone
to stretch life's prison to a wider scope.

Unquiet heart, until that final rest
drum through the tedium of this long today:
trapped in this trickery of mortal quest
throw the sharp instant carelessly away.

TALIESIN: A STRATHCLYDE WINTER

The autumn purple is gone from the hill-slope;
beyond the trees veined on the pale sky,
clouds feather.

Now we have forgotten groves,
abandoned the chase,
like dying men under the raven's eye
we have no cover.

There is no skull in the temple niche,
no blood in the polished cauldron,
no hiss of arrow in the forest trap.
Yet flesh shall not escape mutation.

Our golden toques exchanged for iron collars,
we reach the apex of a latter day, a course
familiar to the prophets.

A white moon rises
beyond the winter ridge;
between the sight and the thought,
the no-man's-land of the real.

——>

The wind howls in the bloody-handed dawn
chilling the same flesh
the same bone-marrow,
compounded of the same dust,

seeded with the same corruption,
repeated through other eyes
that are the same eyes
as long as the race shall live.

I am Taliesin
I am everyman
where past and future meet.

Trees on the bare ridge, bare veins of their summer selves.
White crown of winter once again
on the eternal mountain.

BEACH WALKING

The ocean's whispered promises,
are worthier of an ear than are most others.
After all journeying and useless striving
I come to walk each evening on the shore.

The sea changes: quicksilver to the world's edge
transmutes to lead before the coming storm.

When first I came here seeking,
a child caught up within eternity,
I knew the hand whose cunning fingers
held the bright sun in place; who with a word
could hold the sea back from its ebb and flow.

On this cold twilight shore
the seabird's cry under the greying night
encourages hope.

The soldier as the bullet speeds towards him
may use the word: tomorrow.

SERMON ON MIDLENT SUNDAY

Think when you rise: this day may be your last.
In this night's sleep daylight may never come.
Man that is born of woman has but a short time to live
before the flame's embrace or the clasping yew
forces apart the moulded cluster of dust,
sets free from its earthly matrix the ineffable essence
held in the feeble mantle of the flesh;
a soul caught fleetingly only in arrangement and interval
of colour or sound or word or bronze or stone,
divine impulses that echo the greater work
seen by the blessed within the darkness of silence.

This is the creed that they have sold to you:
to count between the brackets of birth and death
only the known quantity you think is life.
A shuffling up in the conjuror's hat of chance
replaces for you the message of the books.

Now you have bleached your conscience
with the comfortable words of the technicians
Dante and Hieronymus become
teller and painter of a fantasy.
All fear is gone from mutant demon and obscene egg.
'Lasciate ogni speranza':threat of a lovesick poet
recalling in misery a time of happiness.
The damned who fall through the gut of the linked dragons
or slip from the razor-bridge to the lake of fire
are one with the gilded angels and crown of light
mocked as the mad phantom of a fool's eye.
In the inner kingdom, in the darkness of a silent land
are found the substance of dragon and fire and crown.

—>

Kepler looked into the heavens and saw
magical singing stones on a golden cord
swung round the sun's head
noting no random cosmic recreation
but a deliberate game with its own rules.

Now that you sweat before the final folly
of minds built towards life but choosing death,
do not assume the mass extinction of flesh
frees you by common fate from a peculiar judgement.
Though Moloch swallow your children in one gulp
each soul goes singly to the final test.

Because when the blood flows unstaunched
or the slow jagged crab crawls towards death
we call for the small bottle of oblivion;
or when we see beauty turn within a week
into a living agony's changeling mask
we shriek for sorcery or science
or the skilled hands that stitch the fleshy fabric,
restoring the patterns of breath and blood and thought;
that lift the bony trapdoor of the skull
neat as the topshell of a morning egg
to probe the seeming hub of unknown consciousness;
incise and cauterise
the wrinkled offal that you call your soul.
We who have stolen fire and yet replace
the organs wounded by the eagle's talons
are not absolved from final exploration.

--->

After all the peepings and pryings
into the fuming alembic or cathode ray
it does not matter whether the sorcerer
is clothed in a gown of zodiacal signs
or the lab-coat of Eternex Drugs Incorporated.
Their simples remove only the body's pain.
The nostrums for your soul cure only by death.

After the hemlock and the grieving friends
a long infinity of dreamless sleep
or the delightful conversations
within the mansions of a distant house.

But now your mentors leave you
only the option of the final sleep.
The melancholy prince of an abolished father,
you draw out a dull drama without aim,
an infinite regress of cowardly excuses
despising all the ancient arguments.

Despise then also those set in their places.
If in your certainty you smash the saints,
do not replace them with your pinchbeck images.

—->

All art is a parable of eternity.
There is no poet who believes in the victory of dumbness
no painter who sees the eternal death of colour;
Beethoven rises in the fiery flight of eternal music.
The singer hears within the perfect song
therefore such songs must be.
But you have built with strawless bricks of logic
an asylum whose gleaming walls
reflect the barren madness of your thought.

Turn your eyes away from hedging your bets,
the financial pages and the bank-balance,
the hope of tasting a last glutted luxury
before the crab or the coronary,
the cry in the dark: thou fool
tonight thy soul shall be required of thee.

In the dark night that links sleeping and rising
when the whole house is stilled,
seek to discover in that silent time
the lost alternative: in the end all shall be well
all manner of things shall be well.

EXODUS

Aye, we recall the Nile, a wealth of water,
bracelet and breastplate, jewel and chariot,
gold for the gilding of their sweet-spiced dead.
We remember Egypt now, the corn and the oil,
where even a slave could swallow his belly's fill.
What matter the lash, the curse, when hunger was stayed?
Warm nights of satiety and sleep.

A wealth of water and a wealth of wine
that dulled the soul against the passing years.
But here the vision is sharp and the instant bites;
the clear eye seeks the line of a clear horizon.
No mere sobriety has brought this change.

Here scarcity of food and water stretches
skin over ribs that feel the whip no more;
far better hunger here than burn with weals.
More than the shame of slaves has brought this change.

Here we find only wildness of sand and stone.
Even if one should strike a rock with a staff,
turn it to gold, rather it poured forth water.
More than a thirst in the throat has brought this change.

THE POET'S HOUSE

Do not despair that we drift into a dull age.
It has happened before, this contempt of the boor
for those who set words finely upon a page
like bricks in walls they were intended for.
Line upon neat line and new supplies to hand
the lasting houses of the poet-band.

Should they despise the maker and go for dross
the song made for yourself must be the prize.
The poet needs no more. Theirs is the loss
who with a meaner vision blind their eyes.
The sounding walls wherein the maker sings
need no foundation of luxurious things.

MAYA IN THE GARDEN

There's nothing there, they say, but waves in motion.
These coloured caterpillars crunching my green leaves,
ugsome grey slugs whose gluttonous devotion
harden my hatred of such shameless thieves
that I refuse to see all these as one:
a common ghastly mathematic shimmer
that fades to nothing when all's said and done.
Surely if there had been the faintest glimmer
of wisdom's heat from the Laputan sun
that blinds their eyes in cells of stagnant thought
they'd *feel* the champing jaws, the plant's blood run
and view all chequered Being as they ought:
colour, smell, taste, love, hate and good and evil.....
a fitting ambience for God: and devil.

RUSTIC SQUALOR

Down in the birkwood behind the drystone wall
our local Dives dropped his unwanted loot
for the surfeit he can't contain with his Hall.
Not barrel-hoops or holed bins as his grandfather would,
but wall-plugs and fuses, transistors and television tubes,
Wires and condensers and knobs all seeded about.
Now they're switched off they give a louder shout.

SECOND WEDDING

Wine, dancing and laughter.
Who should remember the dead?
There should be happiness thereafter.
Stroking his small fair head,
his mother, they said, replaced;
look to the new life to come.
But he stood back, solemn-faced
thinking on his lost one.

SCOTIA EST DIVISA IN VOCES TRES

Tonight I trauchled around on top of the hill
reflecting on what a stubborn *bodach* (‡) I am,
keeping thrissles and gowans alive in my memory still,
playing treason to God knows what international plan.

Linguistic rebellion should be written in Scots
or Gaelic or Glasgow glottals however broad;
but Scottis, wae's me, is smoort by their pan-loaf plots
and it's no the *luchd-na-Gaidhlig* (†) I ettle tae scaud.

But tonight this flyting came rattling into my head
in the fancy English they've taught me for years to speak;
and although my two other tongues are not quite dead,
yif I yaised ae leid, or tither, *cha bhithinn glic.* (§)
*Is nan robh mi a' bruidhinn Gaidhlig tha fiosam gle mhath
is e 'teuchter' a chanadh iad rium 'san aineolais mor:
canain a shabhail Roinn-eorpa 'san Dorchadas trath
'na cuspair am bial amaideach air son spors.* (‡‡)

--->

All over Alba Gaelic shouts from the stones
to those who have ears to hear, though there's Damn Few left
who can feel their heritage ache like rheumatic bones;
the rest, of all worthy sensations quite bereft,
think if they wag a Lion Flag in your eyes
or stab a synthetic haggis once a year
this this will provide an adequate disguise
for thairms and painches swilled completely clear
of almost anything worthy the native name.
They seem to be chained to shadows that dance in the cave,
(ten light-years away from their Grannie's Hielant Hame)
where they mutter over a mantra of Scotland the Grave.
Is it I who am mad because I will not abandon
the thorns and thistles that made me what I am?
To gain a southern approval or North-British standing
must I swap native spice for International Jam?

The true Scottish essence is none too hard to define
whether you think it a blessing or a blot;
In MacGill-eain and MacDiarmid you'll taste that wine
that runs bitter sweet on the older tongues of the Scot.

Puir auld Dunbar wi mortis conturbat intyre,
twas the mooth-pairchin Inglis that he thocht the mair parfyte;
he lights in my heart a much less comforting fire
than that which Walter Kennedy set alight.....
when Gaelic, he said, should be all true Scotsmen's tongue,
that Scotland it caused to prosper and to spread;
now, ochanee, when our Scottishness is sung
a new tongue stands an old truth on its head.

——>

I'm like a fish that's caught in a dowie doagh;
I wait with impatience and but a little hope
to feel in my gills the freedom of the loch
wherein my urge to swim will be given scope.

You don't even have to beat their forty-percent.....(† †)
all that you need is an ear kept to the ground
if the *siubhal, tuarluath, crunluath* (§ §)that was meant
to keep your gutstrings tuned to a Scottish sound.

(‡) Old Man.
(†) Gaelic speakers.
(§)'I would not be wise'.
(‡ ‡) 'and if I were to speak Gaelic I know well that they would call me a 'teuchter' in their great ignorance....the language that saved Europe in the Dark Ages is a subject for sport in the foolish mouth.'
(† †) This is a reference to the Cunningham Amendment to the terms of the last Devolution referendum.   Forty-percent of the electorate were required to vote for the poll to be legal.   This condition had not been applied to any previous referendum, not even that to join the E.E.C.   Despite this, and false promises made by the opponents of the Bill, the Scots in fact voted for an Assembly.
(§ §) Terms in the Great Music of the pipes.
smoort: smothered.   *ettle:*   try.   *scaud:*   scald.
flyting: poetical polemic.   *yif:*   Middle Scots 'if'.
yaised: used.   *leid:*   language.   *dowie:*   gloomy.
doagh: a salmon cruive, a trap.

FIRST LOVE

Well, that was love, and I remember it,
the hope, the hanging round and the heart's pain,
the coolness, coyness and that off-hand bit
that cut my soul and left me scarcely sane.
Now you are fat and forty and quite plain
I can't imagine what it was I saw
that scented night you passed me in the lane
in that lost sunshine springtime long ago.
Time's fairground mirror to a flatter truth
makes nearer passions by comparing pale;
it's just as well first love does not run smooth
but quits the score with a romantic tale.
I loved you dearly, girl who lived next door;
now, cruel heart, I cannot think what for.

ORPHAN

Severance of the fleshly cord
parts no mother from her sons;
a tougher, ectoplasmic bond
from soul to deathbed soul still runs.

But if this bond be wrenched apart,
the spirit of the orphan drains
from the warm centre of his heart.
Only a phantom flesh remains.

METANOIA

Now not quite old but very far from young,
the heart is calm, late wisdom clears the sight,
retunes the flawed airs once our mouths had sung,
mistaken choice in these last years made right.

For since we cannot walk that old road twice
to right past error in the present mind,
we by the gracious gift of this device
are shriven from the flaws that made us blind.

OLD ENEMIES

Two sour old men waged out their angry feud,
a privet hedge the fortress wall between.
Spillage not quite, but boiling of the blood;
rage in the heart, the guts, all gall and spleen
roused by a hose that sprinkled over far,
weed-flowers on one side rooted on the other;
a dog that entered by a gate ajar
to mark a shrub that never did recover.
Their lives were lived upon a plinth of rage
that ample meals and catnaps scarce abated:
Roland and Oliver grown to surly age
each with the passing years more fiercely hated.

Death thought by taking one to bring relief
but struck again to staunch the other's grief.

A QUESTION FOR EXPERTS

I do not contest, sirs, that apples fall
at two and thirty feet persec persec
or thereabouts, or that they hit the deck
because of some elusive force you call
gravity; or that mathematics fail
to give to modern warriors a basis
for working out to many decimal places
terminal velocity and the angle of trail.
Only a fool would toy with the suggestion
that E might not quite equal MC^2.
Therefore I took some thought before I dared
raise what I feel you'll think a foolish question:
this fruit that falls at its recorded pace,
what hung it up in its appointed place?

SKELETONS

No one who looks over his own shoulder honestly
sees a clear grassy plain. The prospect's strewn
with grinning skeletons of his own past cruelty
that the vulture of time has picked to the bare bone.

Not victims of the axe to the neck's cord,
or tearing nails or thorn about the head;
only the razor-slash of the loveless word,
the indifferent shrug when a smile would have comforted.

___

POLITICAL SYSTEMS

We much disliked the Duke's long nose,
fumed at the squire's rents:
the king's conscripting of our boys
to crowd his battlements.

We made the king a president,
the duke's death we approved;
on the squire's land took residence
once he had been removed.

Soon bored with such democracy
we chafed at one another;
yearned for new aristocracy
such dreariness to smother.

Those who could brew a better beer,
make longer candlesticks,
we raised up to the rank of peer
re-introduced the Rex.

Which much annoyed the peasantry
who rose up from below
with bloody bold unpleasantry
to change the *status quo*.

With rope and axe and guillotine
they whiled long hours away,
claiming that in this new regime
equivalence held sway.

—->

No matter how they fiddled it
we couldn't keep the peace;
corruption always riddled it,
likewise the secret police.

No matter what the system was
some were it wouldn't suit;
however stable seemed the laws
the judges got the boot.

Our towering Utopias
the worm kept tumbling down;
our mooted cornucopias
much easier said than done.

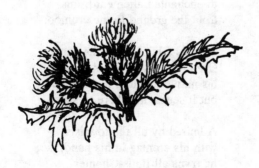

THE ISLE OF INNIS-CHANTER

The isle of Innis-Chanter
far across the western sea
is bathed in Celtic Twilight
by the Tourist Industrie.

For every 'scape's a Landseer
where high on every crag
the Scottish Tourist Board has stuck
a stuffed, but Royal stag.

The women go out waulking
(that's waulking with a 'u'),
sing in a pentatonic wail
as one would have them do.

There every man's a piper
and pibrochs Donal Du,
to enchanted alien eardrums
from the ground to the crunloo.

There's a laird up in the castle
(Eton-Oxbridge, failed B.A.)
his native tongue's not Gaelic
but it seems he's here to stay.

Admired by all the towrists
with his cromag in his hand.....
he owns all Innis-Chanter
except the cockle strand.

––>

Where every tink's a poet,
if not an actual bard,
though not marked as his calling
on his unemployment card.

While high upon a hillock
ringed by Calvinistic mirk
the solitary minister
bawls at an empty kirk.

And calls eternal hell-fire
on the Scottish Towrist Board,
for since they brought the golden calf
the island income's soared.

He deprecates the towrists
who flock in on MacBrayne's
with cars and tents and sleeping bags
and hordes of sinful weans.

The laird, alas, won't stop them,
for higher rents he sees.
Besides the laird's a Piskie (‡)
and prays upon his knees.

So the isle of Innis-Chanter
unlike Lewis or Tiree,
provides quite unashamedly
what the towrist hopes to see.

(‡) *Episcopalian.*

ARMED INTERVENTION

Just before aiming point a comet came
bursting its bomb on the sun's friendly face;
blacked from our sphere his necessary flame.
Ice settled thick, lacking that ancient grace,
freezing the pressured fuel in the pipes,
welding the pilot's fingers to the stick.
For all man's ingenuity and spite
a hidden card may trump his last foul trick.

MODERN HUBRIS

Now that all bowing to the gods has ceased
whereto shall we direct our adoration
needing no services from church and priest?
Seeking new channels for our aspiration
to find a haven for our prayer and art,
no Sistine roof awaits our hymn of paint.
Our unplumbed worship swells within the heart
but stirs no pilgrimage to the shrined saint.

When hell and heaven shrink to one another
the sextant falters and the soundings err.
Even were there new dominions to discover
what measured height have we to guide us there?
Better old haversines upon high seas
than foolproof radar on flat pools like these.

WHO WON?

The irony of all assiduous slaughter:
clangour of bronze on steel, the glutted crows,
is the that deadly disputes rarely matter;
death captures all who dodge the battle-blows.
Since history is the victor's compilation,
whose bones had right or wrong in altercation?

Glory's another word for body-tearing;
all sides recall the justice of their causes,
victor or vanquished none the less despairing.
The weasel treaty waits to break its clauses;
the boasting trumpet, ringing bronze on steel
better no cases; wounds no nation's weal.

Not for mere Marathon we read the Greeks;
the wooden wall's long rotted by the brine;
our latter mind some subtler echo seeks
than carnage, better staged in our own time.
Admire the plated harness Homer burnished,
now that the quarrel's fair excuse has vanished.

BALLANT

Wha meets ye doon the shaw, my son,
while I bide here my lane,
the simmer gloamin nearly din,
aside a bare herth-stane?
Whit limmer bydes yir comin
thro the sheddas daurk and warm?
I fear sae dern a wumman
maun shairlie bring ye herm.

There's nane that hauds me nou, mither
ablo the whuspran trees,
nae sang but the souchan brainch, mither,
that steers i the forenicht breeze;
nocht but a wae-wan face I see
aside the lochan's brink;
it gliffs up frae the deep et me
when I kneel doon tae drink.

doun the shaw: down in the wood. *my lane:* on my own.
simmer gloamin: summer twilight. *limmer:* flighty woman.
bydes: awaits. *sheddas:* shadows. *dern:* secret.
whuspran: whispering. *souchan:* sighing. *brainch:* branch.
steers: stirs. *forenicht:* late evening. *nocht:* nothing.
wae-wan: white with grief. *lochan:* lakelet. *gliffs:* glances.

THREE MEN IN A WOOD

Tomboodie keenly
hears beetle jaws;
ragged unseemly
wilderness grows.

High trunks of timber
fit to be cleared;
counting their number
Mucklewame's cheered.

MacCowl at the back
holds his mind still;
as dry twigs crack,
his spirit fills.

DROUGHT

Do you recall now the grim days of drought,
the dry ear drooping on the withered stalk;
when the lean elders slowly paced around
to see the sweated labour gone for nought?

Long weeks across the waste we made our way
to those wide streams that sweeten that far land,
to find the precious grain was given free
by the lost kinsmen of the open hand.

THE FICKLE FINGER OF FAME

What a great fuss they all made of The Master
for most of his octogenarian life;
he went on extruding stuff faster and faster
to pay for his mistress, his mansion, his wife;
his readings were always a swooning sensation,
well-chosen words in a tightly packed hall;
how could he know that unborn generations
would find nothing much in his matter at all?

Of Puddock the Rhymer they made little fuss;
they starved him to death in an indigent room.
They all said: he's never as clever as us
since all that he's scribbled goes tumty-tum-tum.
But a century on from the flowerless grave
they discovered his papers all smothered in rhyme.....
reviewers and lecturers started to rave
that old Puddock had been in advance of his time.

Unpublished, don't ever dispose of your odes
or booze till your brains dribble out of your ears,
remember success in your lifetime forebodes
ironical laughter in subsequent years.
If your lines don't appear in a leather-bound cover
with raving reviews in the quality press,
discerning posterity may well discover
the genius that shines through your present distress.

THE TURNED FURROW

I sat awhile in their dull schools
I said their prayers and I tried their books,
but letters made me a butt for fools,
so I went away to the plough and stook;
for these are tasks that are better known
to the simple heart and the hands that tend,
but I got nothing but stiff bones
and a grey head at the day's end.

I wrought willing for my whole time,
I gained my bread without trick or lie;
in the leaf's falling and the lapwing's climb
I watched all the brief seasons die.
My field was tilled and my seed sown,
I saw the stalks of my harvest bend,
but I got nothing but stiff bones
and a grey head at the day's end.

Those I loved said they loved me.....
it may well be what they said was true:
love's not a sight that a man can see
like the corn turning or the sloe's blue;
I see my time as I sit alone
specked with ill deeds I cannot mend,
for I have nothing left but stiff bones,
and a grey head at the day's end.

ON THE
APPOINTMENT OF A POET LAUREATE

The Welsh and Gaelic bards were yince weel kent
in histories fir sookan up tae Lairds;
the *filid* and the *pencerdd* aftan penn't
lang screeds fir waddins, daiths and brent new bairns;
well then, why is't that I hae never heard
despite Braemar, Balmoral and Jock Broon
appointment o a eulogistic bard
tae be the Poet Laureate o the Croon?
Nou they've forgot Fifteen and Forty-Five
whit's their excuse fir leavin oot the Celt?
Nou Welsh an Gaelic pech tae stey alive
wad ye no think thet royal herts wad melt
an mak a Celt poetical factotum
tae read doon in Buck Hoose or Winsor Castle?
It canna be they think we hanna got thaim
wha micht wi ilka Royal Occasion wrastle.
It wadna be owre sair tae equal Noyes
or crambo-clink a line as braw as Austin
tae mak gran vairses fir the Royal Ploys
withootan muckle humph-humphan and hoastin.

—->

An whit aboot the leid of Poet Burns?
Is yon no guid eneuch fir thaim the day,
or dae they think Scots bards maun want the harns
syne Wull MacGonnigall hes hud his say?
Man *I* cud dae it aa as weel's the next.....
guid thumpan Standard Habbie wi a rhyme
gin they but tellt me whan the date wes fixt
fir waddins, launchins or the new bairntime.
Jist think hou 'twad delicht the Scottish nation
tae hae a Lallans Laureate bear the gree;
'twad lowse their heids frae thochts o separation
and plans fir Nerra Nationalitie.

————◆————

filid: the ancient Scottish bards. *pencerdd:* the ancient Welsh bards.
Jock Broon: Queen Victoria's Scottish servant. *pech:* gasp.
ilka: each. *crambo-clink:* versify in rhyme. *hoastin:* coughing.
leid: language. *harns:* brains. *Standard Habbie:* A Scots metre.
bear the gree: win the honour. *lowse:* loosen.

THE SUMMER VISITATION

I

Today again our hearts were lifted up,
to watch the clouds grazing their high field,
to feel a summer breeze from the holy hills.

Then we recalled: today will bring the visitors.

The curious visitors who know the formulae,
but cannot change the heart of the barbarian
lost in a stubborn contempt of their new reasons.
They pester us for tales of conversation
with formless spirits on the lonely mountain.

They whisper to their children: *See, this fool*
would rather pay a tithe to savage darkness
than give a useful tax for his improvement.
They will come to laugh again at our simple question:
Have you ever tried to reach those far blue hills?

They counter: *Have you visited our city?*
One cannot move too far from the machines.

Yes, yes; we have been to your city
on a grey morning, taken for social improvement,
to taste the civic values that seem to thrive
among the rusting cranes, the mouldering tower blocks
the grubby ditch of the street, the ruins of banished gods,
the new temples to the tangible metal idols.

——>

Why then did you run?   Did you not see
what we have done to improve the people's position?
Killing the old bosses, digging deeper sewers,
cutting the futile kennings from our learning.....
why did you run back to your huts and herds,
subsistence diet and enforced frugality.....
these strange and savage garments?
You could have been like us.

Because of wood and water, hill and grove.

What comfort in groves, shelter in water,
warmth on a barren hill?

They will come to offer gew-gaws, a sandwich or two
in the hope of coaxing us to sing again
the age-old runes written on hide and bark.

Once, even in the cities, they knew the words,
recited them in the columns of oratories,
argued about their age, compared recensions,
made all their children learn them off by heart.
But that was long before the day of the formulae.

Still, for a time, they recited them in mockery
until they had lost all but the barest fragments
to the skipping songs of children.

But now the children clutch at them and cry:
Tell us what they are saying,
we cannot understand;
we want to know what they are saying.

The adults cannot translate,
they have forgotten the old sounds.

—->

II

If you stand still in the city, listening,
you can hear the faint crumbling of stones and mortar,
tune a fine nostril to the scent of living corpses,
hear in the wind that scrabbles on the walls
the echo of dead demagogues,
a million cries of despair from the high dungeons.

Once there was Athens, now there is only The City.
Buildings that age within the frame of childhood.

Trusting only to pavements
they fear the buzz of flies
disturbed from carrion by a passing foot.

Though they see nothing
beyond the leaves and bark,
they tremble in the groves
but do not speak of it.

As a swimmer tests the water with his toe,
they come here only in summer,
driving proudly up to the reservation.
In summer when the bogs and quagmires are dry,
when the silver crown has vanished from the mountain;
no chill in the probing finger of the wind.

Winter is too hard for the asking of questions.

--->

III

Lured by sirens,
they forget curlew and sanderling,
shellduck and journeying geese.

They are dazed by disharmonies,
deaf to all older songs;
they have abandoned the heart's chorus
for the easy jingle of clowns.

For all the learning,
for all their purged liturgies,
at the end they become men of uncertainty
bolstered by formulae.

Glyphs they have carved upon the wind
they they cannot read with their hearts.

IN HIS OWN COUNTRY

After the concerts in the crowded halls,
the fame that paid him for his noble sound,
he felt a treacherous nostalgic call
to walk again the streets of his own town.

They could not bring themselves to hear him play.
Wrapped in the tribe's conceit they'd slyly grin:
'Big John that never thought to go away
can give a jig or reel that betters *him!'*

FORCED MARCH

Late one evening on the long road
between one camp and yet another,
he passed a village where the torches glowed
and sparks flew upwards in the still weather.

To droning reeds and the tap of drums
a swaying girl danced among the flames;
the jingling gold on her weaving arms
threw him a share of the random gleams.

Embers of days he had thought long dead
kindled once more to remembered pain
for the round arms and the golden head
in a land that he would not see again.

NATURE

I have been too long avoiding groves
of golden sunlight under springtime beeches;
Have walked too long on these bare public roads
where a false prudence barren safety teaches.

I have spent too long gazing in stagnant pools
where the eye's prisoner to a surface sheen
that mirrors vanity and flatters fools
and lures desire from where the spring runs clean.

DRINKS

Early, there are the pleasures of the senses;
later remain the pleasures of the mind,
which in their turn, have certain recompenses.
Like cider-pips-and-all before good wine.

Now, even though my palate's more discerning
my youthful taste's not quite beneath the pall;
I sip my clear thin wine to drown a yearning
for the old cloudy scrumpy, pips and all.

LISTED HOUSE: STEWARTRY

After the laird had built him this grand house
stepping foul by the ford the heir was drowned,
in the small hours after a night's carouse;
a month went by before the corpse was found.

The old mansion wears its three hundred years;
preserved windows look on the tidy lawn;
down by the riverside a grey mist clears,
trees weep for old shades against the dawn.

Walking early beneath the first bird song,
feel how the morning fills with summer joy;
look down to the ford where a step went wrong,
where weeds tangled the throat of the singing boy.

NURSEMAIDS AND SOLDIERS

The Duke of Dedleigh's Horse Hussars
wore jackets bright with lace and spangles.
In twilight swaggerings through the park
you'd hear their spurs and medals jangle.

The nursemaids eyed them with delight;
they swooned and drooped with admiration,
arranged that their off-duty nights
should coincide for assignation.

But sabres sliced the handsome skulls;
guns blew strong legs off at the thighs,
while master craftsmen, rich but dull
enjoyed the nursemaids' midnight sighs.

Bright trumpets ringing in the head,
the fancy coat, the prancing steed
recruit replacements for the dead.
A sober stock maintains the breed.

FRAME

The blind men at the Cosmic Snooker Match
had come to hear the music of the spheres.
No subtler tune came to their waiting ears
than random clicks whose code they could not catch.

Their sighted friends who understood the game
tried to explain the spectrum of the score,
but a reduction from all five to four
proscribed a faith when hue was but a name.

LOCHAR WATTER

Heich biggin an heich maitter
warld's misure o walth's fee
in the lang wuid by the Lochar Watter
yon's whaur I wad raither be.

Bricht siller and gowden pletter
the purpie claith an the cramosie,
in the lang wuid by the Lochar Watter
yon's whaur I wad raither be.

Prood palace and lear's letter,
faur citie and fremit sea,
in the lang wuid by the Lochar Watter
yon's whaur I wad raither be.

The wearie years dinna bield better
frae auld myndans that winna dee,
in the lang wuid by the Lochar Watter,
the ae place that I canna be.

heich: high. *cramosie:* crimson. *lear:* learning.
fremit: foreign. *bield:* protect. *myndans:* memories.

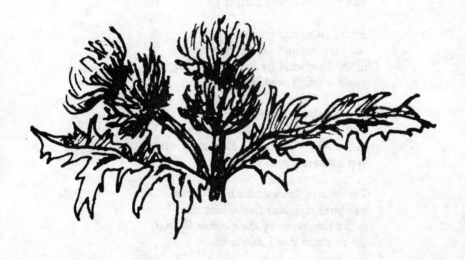

MEMO. TO CHRIS GRIEVE.

In March 1984, the Regional Planning Committee of Dumfries and Galloway decided by six votes to five to refuse planning permission for a memorial sculpture at Langholm, the birthplace of Chris. Grieve (Hugh MacDiarmid). The design for the memorial had been chosen by an authoritative panel of judges from an international selection of entries. The work was to be executed by a local artist, a commission worth £17,000. The site for the memorial had been donated by the Duke of Buccleugh. One of the councillors responsible for the decision said that the memorial would be 'an intrusion', and that he would not approve of an Oxo advertisment on the site! Another councillor said that when the Committee visited the site, it was a foggy day and "you couldn't see a thing."

In the *Dumfries and Galloway Standard and Advertiser,* the local paper, John Aitkenhead wrote: *'Intrusion indeed! MacDiarmid's whole challenge was an intrusion on the half-dead, almost wholly defeated, colonialised state of Scottish society. His poetry was a rude intrusion, a magnificent intrusion, into the complacent acceptance of the Scottish language as something inferior to so-called Standard English. And now we gladly recognise the result of that intrusion, that new vision of his in the twenty's of this century. It is, in a word, the Scottish Literary Renaissance, nothing less. And aren't we grateful.'*

The two following poems were written in black anger at that decision by the Planning Committee.

MEMO. TO CHRIS CHRIEVE

Dear Chris, I know that where great poets go
after their troubled lives, you're surely there,
and mankind's meanness is revealed to you
more clearly than it was when you were here.
High on Parnassus, though you may not care.....
please listen to my angry, earthly voice
amend for Councillor Bumpkin and his ploys.

I do not know if Bumpkin is a Scot;
one can't gauge Scottishness just by a name.....
his actions seem to indicate he's not:
surely no Scot would play in such a game.....
scoring own-goals to Scotland's bitter shame?
But if he be a Scot, I take it hard—
watching his efforts to affront a bard.

Of course, he hasn't read a word you wrote.....
nor one small line of verse since leaving school;
knows even less of sculpture than a goat.....
hums, haws and ifs and buts are Bumpkin's tool
with which he seeks to babble and befool.
It does not serve dull Bumpkin's clownish turns
to honour Scotland's greatest bard since Burns.

—->

Not one of Langholm's sons could hold a candle
to you, Chris Grieve, in the poetic art.
Although you once dug up a bit of scandal,
do such old tales still form a living part
of graveyard grudge borne in a vengeful heart
because an ancient, saucy tale you proved
against his grannie's cousin twice removed?

No, no, I'm certain yon old spite is dead.....
I KNOW that Bumpkin doesn't live in Langholm;
besides, I'm sure your work he hasn't read —
and Scottish poets, why, this dunce would hang 'em;
a sculptor's mallet, chiselling and banging
is not a skill with which our clod's familiar.....
which makes His Bumptiousness look even sillier.

Bumpkin has swayed the meeting in his favour
to damn your memory in the name of 'planning';
that's his excuse, but I dislike its flavour.....
I smell the stink that lies beneath the banning.
SIX VOTES TO FIVE!.....you nearly made the running!
How the great world that lives beyond Doon Hame
will heap up scorn on each dissenting name.

Doon Hame: Dumfries.

WHA JEEDGES PIGS,
JEEDGES SCULPTURE TAE.

Ma hert fair stouns wi scunner
et puir Scotland's latest hap:
for they'll hae nae sculpture yonner
on the Lang Toun's braid hill-tap,
syne a wheen wee douce Doonhamers
hae damned yon brawlik plan.....
led by the neb in chaumers
by a fermin Inglishman.

Et least whan Rabbie hud been cauld
for twintie year an mair,
they gied his banes anither hauld.....
yon marble rickle there;
nou eident chiels wha sculptures scart
wi skeelie dunts an digs,
fin fouth o critics for their Art
(whan they're no cuiterin pigs).

Chris Grieve, yir mindin's in sic wark
that tholes lik airn or stane
the gowkit gant, the spitten smirk
o whilk sic tykes are fain.
Ye wha MacDiarmid's cairn wad cowp
and spit in Scotland's face.....
a sculpture o a grumphie's dowp
sud mark yir ain disgrace.

Stoun: thump. *scunner:* disgust. *hauld:* shelter.
rickle: pile. *eident:* clever. *fouth:* plenty.
gowkit gant: cuckoo stare. *spitten smirk:* spiteful grip.
grumphie: pig. *dowp:* backside.

A PACKET
OF BROADSHEETS,

Being:

Sawnie's Complaint.

Crionadh Foghlam Na H-Alba.
Or
The Crynan O Scotia's Lear.
Or
The Decline of Scottish Learning.

Another Letter To Lord Byron.

The Jolly Trimmers

Or

Love Of Slavery.

SAWNIE'S COMPLAINT

Dan aoireil air an sgath-san nach tuig Gaidhlig no Albais; na's fior-Ghaidheal sibh, gabhaibh mo leisgeul.

A blaud scrievit in heich Inglis fir sic as hae nae grup o the twa aulder leids; gin ye ken ither or baith I'm shair ye'll no tak the strunts.

A Broadsheet in plain English for those who cannot read our other two languages.

Those bards who used to carp in five-stressed lines
are out of favour in our clever times:
image and symbol in free verses clashing
put Pope's and Dryden's manner out of fashion.
Wild George, Lord Byron, that reluctant Scot,
gains scanty laurels from this modern lot.
Yet still I'm tempted, when compelled by rage
to crambo-clink out venom by the page:
though rhyming couplets may be out of style
they're much the best mode for satiric bile.
Scots verse or English is another matter....
no traitor I if I should choose the latter,
for modern Scottie has but little knowledge,
(brainwashed in school and then wrung out in college)
of his own tongues; but most can speak and read
(with some small Scottish quirks) the English leid.
Lallans and Erse, alas, I must abandon
such English as I have I'll make a stand on.

—>

Bones of dead Picti on Mons Graupius hill
if in those rough-bounds something of you still
mingles where skiers on your hard-won heights
learn to appreciate the rich delights
of Scottish hills, Scotch drink and NORTH SEA oil
at which the natives are allowed to toil,
being set from under Scottish nebs to drag
our greedy London master's Scottish swag
while rusting Scottish shipyards beg a tithe
of millions spent ten miles round Rotherhithe.....
look on this craggy, rocky knuckle-end
that once you sought in freedom to defend,
now the last vassal of the English race,
our people shameless in their own disgrace.
Your warning stands today, brave Pictish chief....
they make a wilderness and call it peace.

What other land's gulled twice in each decade
by jobbers in the Parliamentary trade
who promise us HOME RULE before elections
quite unashamed by subsequent defections?
These lie to bolster what they call tradition.....
to sit by turns in Rule or Opposition,
so deeply sunk in great affairs of state
(that to all nations but their own relate)
unmindful of mean street and bleak hillside
where their constituents miserably bide.
Some pretend Redness, prate of John MacLean
dead long enough to make that safe again;
others, the purest Unionist True Blue
boast PRIVATE ENTERPRISE IS BEST FOR YOU!
when not a TITHE.....a THIRD they take away.
'Invest the rest in industry,' they say.
Don't spend the lot on horses, drink and fags.....
aspire to riches, Sawnie, from your rags.'   ——>

165

Ye hypocrites who from the sale of beer
advance from brewer's tub to ermined peer;
ye statesmen who from taxing Indian Weed
pay for the nuclear death ye claim to need;
ye London companies who gorge and swill
the profits from each Scottish whisky still.....
pretend that Sawnie's common vices grieve you,
but don't expect a wise man to believe you.

Ye Socialists, who plough your private farms,
who far from slumland bask in rural charms,
how easily you learn High Tory practice
of subsidising pigs from poor men's taxes.
Sad, honest John MacLean, long laid to rest,
damned by the rich but still by poor men blessed,
owned little land but prison floor and grave.
Enjoy your fields, but don't blaspheme the brave.

Poor Sawnie, he's too dull to see your actions,
but keeps on voting for your tawdrie factions,
and sends you down to London each five years
to further your political careers;
a time for Tweedledum, then Tweedledee:
This year you govern, Dum, then next year me.....
Third party interference we can smother
by public fawning over one another,
resolve our pseudo-quarrel for a while
until the errant voters we beguile
by preaching that THREE PARTIES WILL NOT DO!.....
we'll win the stray sheep back to me and you.
Then, every time some faction gets together
dull Taff and Simple Sawnie to deliver,
we'll think up tricks to cover with derision
the thought that they be heard on television;
we'll hit them low in propaganda clinches
by simply starving them of column-inches.
Of course, we needn't feel much apprehension.....
trust to the Celtic genius for dissension,
for any group composed of two-score Scots
will soon dissolve to forty different lots: —->
who's Left, who's Centre, radical or Right.....
soon the main issue is forgotten quite.....

Thus barren Government and Opposition
preserve a worn-out Cat-and-Dog tradition
forever wrangling in a mock debate.....
fake democrats within a huckster state.

Fake democrats, you say!   Is that quite fair?
Mother of Parliaments, proud name you bear
but seem to favour most those southern sons
who in all battles bear the biggest guns.
Besides, you've found a way of foiling fools:
when things don't suit *your* boys, you change the rules.
A referendum's not one when it's bent
to cunning humbug of two-score percent.
Though the whole island sees the count was rotten,
give it a month or so and it's forgotten.

When the day's lost to a true democrat,
Mother of Parliaments, he does not rat
or cheat, or fiddle numbers in a Bill
to foil by Party Tricks the Peoples' Will.
Those who by sharpers' trimming gain their point,
weaken your bones, Old Dame, in every joint.

When Scotland's Parliament, untimely ripped
from Scotland's womb, was south to London shipped,
a carlin who observed the sorry ploy
of this foul closure, said with little joy:
When Scots chiels sate in ben yon Scottish Hoose
and wi oor polity played fast and loose,
stanes roon their heids a Scottish haund micht caa....
but south tae London toun's an unco thraw.....

––>

Today, as if to baulk the Scottish will,
we send ambitious placemen Southward still
whose seeking natures thrill with every mile
the night express gains southward of Carlisle,
glad once again to crawl within the womb
of England's dear old mother, Scotland's tomb.
See how they mix there, affable, urbane.....
happy to be in London once again.....
discoursing loudly on the World's Affairs
flowing with hope of ministerial chairs.
Quite, quite forgetful of poor Scotland's losses
they tug their forelocks to their English bosses.

And Scotland?   Once a land in UNION joined,
finds all her ancient privilege purloined;
the worthy pride of an old sturdy nation,
reduced by clowns beneath that honoured station,
while London City Gents, fat on our bounty,
equate our kingdom with an English county.

See in the lounge there, Toomboodie M.P.
who burned to set the Scottish workmen free,
become a trumpet of uncertain sound,
in hopes of office when his turn comes round.
Foul, leaking slums in Scotland, once his care
still leak, and still are foul, and will be there
for him to shout about before elections
and blame them all on Mucklewame's defections.

Mucklewame, champion of Free Enterprise.....
visions of ermine grandeur glaze *his* eyes.....
in late night queues at Scottish aerodromes
he dreams of long week-ends in stately homes.....
of Honours Lists, and how to gain an entry
to permanent acceptance by The Gentry.....
while banishing all thoughts of Caledonia
a place (though full of oil) a great deal stonier.

--->

See poor MacCowal, Scotsman to the bone,
eager to serve, who bites his nails at home.
Patriot John Bull's the noblest thing on earth.....
but patriot Scots are thought of little worth.

The Scottish name provokes a London sneer.
(All greater Scots, you see, are *English* there.....
Fleming, Clerk Maxwell, Baird or Davie Hume,
the English pantheon gladly gives them room)
but try to be a *Scottish* politician
who seeks improvement of his land's position.....
whispered ill-will soon rises to a roar
while Scottish hirelings rush to swell the score.
For True Democracy, it seems is not
allowed as birthright to the decent Scot.

'Each to his own' would seem an honest quote
but England keeps her hand round Scotland's throat;
while Scotland rots and bleeds her wealth and brains
her idiot offspring sing North British strains:
mean 'kenned-his-faither' numbskulls swank and stump
their brainless envy round each parish pump.....
such Scots as ponder on the Scottish name
slink to the hills, or drink to hide their shame.

The rest, to London bound in drunken batches,
bawl out their patriotic zeal at football matches,
suck sweets and read historical romances
or prance in too-long kilts in country dances;
deer-stalking dunces crawl through heather clumps
past shattered pulp-mills, weed-grown smelter-dumps.....
Tweed-skirted dames, shod with expensive brogues,
sell home-made jam to purchase votes for rogues:
while lounge-bar lefties, dressed to fit the role
mouth dialectic to confound the prole.
At Conference the clay-foot statesmen mention
Planned Devolution that they've no intention
(once sat in Westminster) of ever ceding,
since after all, they're likely to be needing
our heather acres till the oil runs dry.....
or they arrange our nuclear Goodbye.

CRIONADH FOGHLAM NA H-ALBA

THE CRYNAN O SCOTIA'S LEAR

THE DECLINE OF SCOTTISH LEARNING

DAN MACARONACH LE FOCLAIR
AGUS EADAR-THEANGACHADH

AE MACARONIC BALLANT WI GLOSSARIE
AND OWRESETTAN

A MACARONIC BALLAD WITH GLOSSARY
AND TRANSLATION

SGRIOBH GU FIOSACH FIREOLACH
A SHEANCHAS IS A GCAITHREIM.
Fionnlagh Mac an Aba.   C.1500.

1..... After the tumult and the shouting died
under the vaulted ceilings of Dunedin
where vain and empty heads had swooned and sighed
on ploughman-bards who showed such noble breeding,
you chose auld claes and parritch in the west.
That for our sakes, was surely for the best.

2..... Hired to the Whigamores, uneasy pax
you tholed, and scribbled in a Doon-Hame vennel;
collected the hated Hanoverian tax
up to your fecket in the Solway channel.
Wherever your heart was, Rab, it was not here
chasing stags of the soul in a gauger's gear.

3..... Now, annually, some pan-loaf speaking ass
gives a few ill-learned lines of yours the air,
seeks with an empty speech to bring to pass
Scotland's resurgence for three hours a year,
while big-wamed Baillies bawl out 'Scotland Yet',
till the bleak dawn, when jaded minds are set

4..... to the prudent task of keeping the balance right;
all Scotchness fettered in a toadie's heart
in a land that smothers under bad advice.....
first-fruits of London's governmental art,
for Mr. Sunday-Scotland your new M.P.
whose party place outbids democracy.

5..... Our Scottish leids are openly despised;
in bookish cliques there's no debate upon
what tongue will best achieve the Glittering Prize:
concord of London critic, Oxbridge don.
Gaelic and Scots the *maestri* now omit
from New Licht seminars on 'Scottish' Lit.

—-->

6.....   There's chiels that scrieve in Scots baith real an Plastic
some read the ane an blether in the ither;
a wheen micht gie ye Gaelic gin ye ask it
or Beurla Mor withooten muckle bother.
But whaur the 'Scottish' literati gether
it's seenil ye'll hear ocht but Inglis cletter.

7.....   Agus an diugh, ged is gle bhochd ar saoghal
tha Ruaraidh againn agus Somhairle Mor
a sgriobhas *lingua Scotorum* le gaol
an teanga 'thuirt an Cinneideach bu choir
a bhith aig gach fior-Albannach mar chainnt:
am measg na graisge sud is beag an t-seans.

8.....   An gentil skeelie Deorsa mac Iain Deors'
nou ane wi Alasdair an Duncan Ban
scrievit in three leids wi an eident force
fir sic-like Scots as in three leids kin scan.
Dh'innis e dhuinn: *'son airgead no ni.....
na treig do thalamh dhuthchais'*.....ochan i!

9.....   Nou that great Mac a' Greidhir's in the box
(hou monie ken the Gaelic fir his name?)
the fleggit aidders slide oot frae the rock
tae set aboot their Scotland-smoorin game
turn Cockney cac-nam-bo oot by the quair
tae cheinge auld Alba intil Scotlandshire.

10.....   It sud rise birses when some London scunner
tellied tae ilka Scottish but-an-ben
caa's ye PROVINCIAL!   Some wee southran wunner
blethran o Kultur efter News at Ten.
We maun be scrievin literate defiance
no snirtan in a cultural compliance.

––—>

11..... Mac Mhaighstir Alasdair abandoned school,
        threw off the scholar's gown for belted tartan,
        supporting not so much the princely fool
        as a more desperate cause he'd set his heart on
        (how difficult for some the honest thought
        that Scotland should be governed by the Scot.)

12..... And skulking back at last when all was over
        to bitter lurking in Dunedin's streets,
        he managed still such spirit to recover
        as made new songs to fit poor Scotland's needs.
        But Sons of Scotlandshire, to our great loss
        burned his new verses at the Mercat Cross.

13..... A process that still works for them you'll find
        for Scots and Gaelic writing find no other
        echo within the dull North British mind
        than a mere envious desire to smother
        all that's most Scottish in this dowie land.
        Our sad dead bards look on a weary band.....

14..... of poetasting dunces whose intention
        (guided by what's the fashion in the South)
        bows only to what southern critics mention.
        the *filid* down at heel and down at mouth
        write their wersh lines in gurlie native jargon
        to help them thole the miserable bargain.

—->

15..... Gif London's approbation's aa they want
oor Scottish leids til Grub Street canna help thaim,
let cultural ken-betters gaup and gaunt,
in crambo-clinkan duans I maun skelp thaim,
raxin oot whiles tae grup ane by the hauch
and dreg his grunzie frae yon fremit trouch.

16..... If, unregairdit, Scotland's leids maun perish,
by misbehadden learlessness coost doon,
yon southran souch thet they sae muckle cherish
wull et the lest oor native mainners droon.
Let aa they scrieve be wyce and gleg and modish,
there's ae thing siccar, it wull no be Scottish.

NOTES.
The two Gaelic lines by Finlay MacNab are:
'Write knowledgeably and with true learning of their history and culture.'

1. *Dunedin:* Edinburgh. *auld claes an parritch:* down to earth.

2. That Burns was a Jacobite sympathiser is obvious from his poetry and correspondence. *Doon-Hame:* Dumfries, presumably for the habit of natives exiled to Glasgow and Edinburgh in talking of their native place. *gauger:* Customs official. *fecket:* waistcoat.

3. To speak *'pan-loaf'* is Glasgow slang for affected speech.

4. *big-wamed:* big-bellied.

——>

174

5. *leids:* languages. *'New Licht'* was the epithet given to a faction in the Kirk.

6. *chiels:* fellows. *scrieve:* write. *Plastic Scots:* the kind of universal and historical mixture of Scots used by Hugh MacDiarmid. *blether:* prattle. *wheen:* a few. *Beurla Mor:* Standard Southern English. *seenil:* seldom. *ocht:* anything. *cletter:* chit-chat.

7. *'and today although poor is our state / we have Ruaraidh* (Derick Thomson) *and great Sorley* (Maclean) *who will write the tongue of the Scot with love / the language that Kennedy said ought to be the speech of all true Scots. / Among yon crowd there's little chance of that.*
The Kennedy referred to is Walter Kennedy of Culzean (see *'The Flyting of Dunbar and Kennedy')* in Ayrshire, who defended his native Gaelic of Carrick against the attack of Dunbar, c.1500.

8. *Deorsa MacIain Deorsa* is the by-name of the late George Campbell Hay, who wrote splendid poetry in Gaelic, Scots and English. *Alisdair* (MacDonald) and *Duncan Ban* (MacIntyre) are 18th cent. Gaelic poets. Alisdair is mentioned again in Verses 11 and 12. *eident:* earnest, diligent. The Gaelic is: *He told us, for money or any other thing "do not forsake your native land".....alas!'* The phrase in quotation marks is taken from G.C. Hay's own poem of that name.

9. *Mac a' Ghreidhir:* Grieve. Christopher Murray Grieve, who wrote under the pen-name of Hugh MacDiarmid. *fleggit:* scared. *aidders:* adders. *smoorin:* smothering. *cac-nam-bo:* bullshit. *quair:* quire.

10. *birses:* bristles, nape-hairs. *scunner:* object of contempt or disgust. *blethran:* prattling. *'Kultur'* is deliberately used for 'culture' to indicate that ignorant imperialism which pushes its own culture at the expense of others. *maun:* must. *snirtan:* sniggering.

—->

11. Mac Mhaighstir Alasdair is the by-name of the poet Alasdair MacDonald, mentioned above. He spent some time in the University of Glasgow, became a schoolmaster and later a captain in the Jacobite Army. He managed to escape after Culloden, returning a few years later to Edinburgh where he started to write and publish Jacobite songs. These were, it is said, seized and burned by the common hangman. *Plus ca change.....*

13. 'North British' is a pejorative term, referring to anglicised Scots. *dowie:* gloomy, doleful.

14. The *filid* were the highest order of ancient Gaelic poets. They were men of considerable culture and education as opposed to the less cultured 'bards'. *wersh:* sour, bitter. *gurlie:* surly, sullen. *'The miserable bargain'* refers to the Treaty of Union.

15. Scotland is full of 'cultural ken-betters' who, without the benefit of Scots or Gaelic set themselves up as the *cognoscenti* of Scottish letters. Consider the fate of the critic of Homer who knew no Greek!
gaup an gaunt: gape and stare. *crambo-clinkan duans:* rough rhyming verses. *skelp:* slap. *raxin:* reaching.
haugh: hock. *an dregs his grunzie frae yon fremit trouch:* and drags his pig's snout from that alien trough.

16. leids: languages. *misbehadden:* unseemly. *learlessness:* lack of education. *coost:* cast (pret.) *southran souch:* southern style. *wyce an gleg:* wise and witty. *ae thing siccar:* one thing sure.

176

ANOTHER LETTER TO LORD BYRON.

Readers will recall that Byron was so aroused to fury by a review in the EDINBURGH REVIEW of March 1808 that he wrote a satiric diatribe against Scotch Reviewers in general and Jeffrey the editor in particular, and damned in his verses all those whom the Edinburgh Reviewers praised.   It is often forgotten that Byron himself once pointed out that he had been born half a Scot and bred a whole one.   It will also be remembered that W.H. Auden whiled away some of his time in Iceland writing a Letter to Lord Byron.   Writing letters to phantoms may be as vain an occupation in all senses of the word as publishing Broadsheets. The only possible excuse is that a third party will be amused.

If from the slopes of some remote Parnassus
you deign to look upon this mortal coil
whereon our modern insolence surpasses
the dead conceits that brought you to the boil.....
forgive me if I burn the midnight oil
converted by the Electricity Board
who've made it cheaper, though the price has soared,

to write you, George, (I lay aside the title,
and call you George, or maybe Mister Gordon)
I feel that Scottish surname's somehow vital
when Scotland's quirks I'm keeping watch and ward on.....
I know such antics make you yawn with boredom.....
You may well ask me how I have the face to,
but I don't know who else to put my case to.

––>

'Born half a Scot,' you said, 'and bred a whole one.....'
Harrow and Cambridge smothered out the Scot.....
a process that has ceased now to appal one.....
the common practice of our posher lot.....
whether their land's heredit'ry or bought,
against our thistly ways they take precaution
and send their scions southward for brainwashing.

Of course your Scottish chromosomes still rankled
just like my own (though maybe not with pride)
since with our Scotch reviewers once you tangled
when they had given your stuff a bumpy ride;
but whether critics praise you or deride.....
it's better far they should provoke your rages
than send back manuscripts and slight your pages.

I share with you, I must confess the fault,
a certain penchant for sardonic stanzas
that throw an acid literary salt
among those delicate extravaganzas
that get in print; prosodian Sancho Panzas
to show that windmills rarely giants frame.....
or windbag scribblers, for that's just the same.

I've read your howls of anger and frustration
when northern critics fuelled your distresses.
At least you had achieved some publication;
Proud Scotland then possessed some printing presses.
Now though some inky saints remain to bless us.....
grey Edimbro the large founts all abandon,
and with all other trimmers flee to London.

-->

I live upon a distant western moor
where Gaelic names adorn both farm and mountain;
heather, not roses, grows around my door,
the loch's my spring, not far Castalia's fountain.....
you'll hear the grouse whirr, see the roe deer bounding,
hear the sheep bleat, the shaggy cattle bellow,
but seldom meet a literary fellow.

Forgive me, Mister Gordon, a frustration
that makes me scribble to your wispy ghost;
a crank who still regards the Scottish Nation
as still extant, though very nearly lost.....
some think it merest history, at most.
Clever chaps find me (don't you think it sad)
a scoundrel patriot — gone slightly mad.

The country's full of nineteenth centuries Tories
(though Fabian Socialists are still around)
our dear old Liberals tell the ancient stories
to bore me with Westminster's hollow sound.
Every four years they cover the same ground,
impervious to yawns and snores and sighs
they deafen Scotland with the same old lies.

So leave the politics to politicians.....
since statesmen show once in a thousand years;
let fools bask in Utopian superstitions
and smother Hansard in their boos and cheers.....
we buy their steaks and subsidise their beers,
but whether sour or lyric, bland or mordant.....
we both think versifying more important.

--->

Some Scottish scribblers indicate direction,
leave them to swing, their noses all point south,
since west and north they think have predilections
for strange old words that rumble in the mouth
and sound barbaric, weird, arcane, uncouth.....
the Great Plook does not like these very much
preferring Oxbridge-Fleet-Street prose and such.

From time to time I have to look for reasons
why Scotchness I should think of such import.....
when I myself might take up those same treasons
adopted by the southward-seeking sort;
aim at the kind of English heard at court.....
paint Sawnie as a flag-day Aberdonian
and damn the guts of all thing Caledonian.

My Lord, when you'd won south from Aberdeen
despite those verses on Dark Lochnagar.....
back home in Scotland you were seldom seen
where all those Calvinistic bogies are.....
One touch of Scotchness may from fame debar;
the literary list-compiling lot
rarely point out that your were half a Scot.

But then, why should they? If you're good enough
to gain the ear of the great world outside
they'll make you English.....cockney-fy your stuff
like Davie Hume; gulp down all your Scottish pride
you'll gain a reputation far and wide.
Damn Scottishness!   accept the English order.....
you never need look back across the Border.

--->

There, George, I'm off again, both stern and wild
perfervidum ingenium (‡)and all that.....
but is this really patriotism or bile?
Scotch cockernonie or a Luton hat,
or wreath of laurel on the forehead sat.....
toga or Gaulish cloak or philabeg,
are bards not bards in socked or buskined leg?

The SCOTSMAN's filled with letters every day.....
indignant over England's usurpation,
where each one points out his own private way.....
how to escape from southern domination.
I must confess, not without some elation
I watch these mangy Scottish birses rise.
It brings, at times, salt tears into my eyes.

What is this Scottishness they love so much?
They don't like bishops, only moderators.....
though when they did have bishoprics and such
our poor old nation had a better status.
Are we held up on Calvin's cold afflatus?
Did not the Butcher burn the *Piskie* steeple,
lock up *their* ministers, and hang *their* people? (†)

Or else they say: we have the Scottish Law
(only judiciary, there's no legislature)
and think this gives them some great cause to crow.....
it gives the place a more official nature.
But when *The Eagle* sank upon *The Creatures* (§)
of English Admirals they asked permission
before they dared set up a Scotch Commission.

—->

Some say, my Lord: at least we have our language.....
I wonder, now, what language do they mean?
Our plebs pronounce a sandwich as a *sangwich*.....
does this from Englishness divorce them clean?
Scots they think common, Gaelic's seldom seen,
save when it's daubed on traffic signs by CEARTAS..... (‡ ‡)
even there the crafty Cambrians outsmart us.

Of course at threescore I'm a bit oldfashioned
with rhyming diatribes that nearly scan;
my whole sour soul with Scottishness impassioned.....
a trait fastidious poetasters damn.
Sometimes I nearly rhyme, like metric psalms......
there's no old trick that in my verse is stinted.....
which makes it difficult to get them printed.

Some say my stuff's a bit like tinker piping.....
all on one tune, a fault I will confess to;
I'm thirled to bitter Caledonian griping.....
a broadsheet bullying in the end addressed to
converts; although I know it would be best to
abandon rhymes like this and court Euterpe.
(The rhymes for her are rather less than thirty.)

Last night I read a life of Robert Burns.....
for all his faults I still admire the fellow.....
polemicising Scot, and bard by turns
from sweet song to the patriotic bellow.....
a trait that hard experience failed to mellow.
Goaded by fools and patronised by snobs
and forced by failing crops to sue for jobs.

--->

How did he manage to maintain the stance
of Scottishness in life and of the work?
'Don't write in Scots,' they said, 'you won't advance.....
They'll read you no more that they would a Turk.
Eschew such words as *crannreuch, blate* and *mirk*
stell, sheuch and *scunner* score out from your list;
say: hold and ditch and frost and sky and mist.'

I know, my Lord, you hated Scotch Reviewers.
Hydra, I think you called them in your spleen;
the lines they praised you thought fit for the sewers;
those bards whose feathers Jeffrey chose to preen
not to be heard, you held, or even seen
in hard black print on any decent page.
And yet I sigh for that Athenian age.....

When bards in Southwell were so stung to ire
by publishers upon the Canongate,
as wish to roast them in satiric fire;
could we but find again that blessed state
when English bards on Scotch opinion wait;
when scribblers paid such earnest close attention
to anything in Scotland worth a mention.

Is anything in Scotland worth a mention?
Where Fleet Street rules and London presses rumble
to southern tastes all scribes must pay attention
to see the bright coins through their fingers tumble.
Poor Simple Sawnie really mustn't grumble
if when a laureate bard they must appoint.....
all Scottish noses are put out of joint.

--->

Grecian Lord Byron, is it not unjust,
that scribblers living close to Piccadilly
now that our native printing presses rust,
should think our land barbarian, hairy, hilly,
tartan-and-whiskified and cold and silly.....
object to native words like *theek* and *thole* (§ §)
because *they* did not hear them when at school.?

A few bold warriors at their ledgers squinting
in hope the black will just outscore the red
go in for risks like publishing and printing
such lines as boom within the Scottish head.
Perfervidum ingenium, nearly dead,
from brave small presses gets an upward hitch.....
but patriot poetry-printers don't get rich.

Even the stuff *you* wrote that rhymed and scanned
won't do in London now; your bold Don Juan
from London lists would certainly be banned
and like the rest of us you'd face black ruin.
For clear-as-day type bards there's nothing doing
if you've no bent for crossword-clue obscurity
an ear for form and content are no surety

against the talentless, the dreary dunce
who knows no prosody and makes no sense
but haunts each London literary lunch,
wagging a sheaf of verses,dull and dense
and looking interesting, strung out and tense;
if once he gets some pundit to protect him
the editors are frightened to reject him.

—–>

So then, my Lord, hater of Scottish presses,
of Scotch reviewers, northern criticasters.....
consider the Scotch scribbler's new distresses
now Grub Street scribblers have become our masters.
Greater by far, Lord George, are our disasters
than any long-dead Edinburgh Review
which failed to give you what you thought your due.

That's it, my Lord.   To finish I'll make haste.
Your ghost, I'm sure must be much madder still
to know the arbiters of every taste
live in that five-mile-stews round Ludgate Hill.
Should Jeffrey's thin wraith skulk behind you still
he'll grin and smirk to see you get the blues
now London writes, prints, reads, mere Parish News. († †)

—>

NOTES.

‡   *'Perfervidum Ingenium Scotorum'* or as Buchanan put it *'Scotorum praefervida ingenia'.....*the ardent temperament of the Scots.

†   See *The Scottish Church and Nation'* Donaldson, G.

§   The *Iolaire* (Gaelic: Eagle) sank on the Beasts of Holm on January 1st, 1919. Many Lewismen who had survived the Great War were lost in that disaster.

‡ ‡   *CEARTAS:* Justice. This is a body dedicated to the obtaining of official status for Gaelic, the oldest Scottish tongue, whose speakers labour under certain disadvantages as regards their own language in their own country. It is almost inconceivable that this should be the case in any allegedly civilised State.

§ §.   The word *'thole'*, which is still in common use in Scotland (and in northern England) was objected to by a critic in a London 'quality' newspaper as an archaism in a novel written by a Scot. (Summer 1984)

† †   Anyone north of The Wash cannot but be astounded by the ingrowing parochialism of the 'quality' London press as far as internal coverage is concerned. It might well be described as London and Overseas News.

Glossary of Native Scots words (in order of appearance.)
The Great Plook: William Cobbett (1762—1835) referred to London as *"The Great Wen'....the monster, called ...the metropolis....'* A *'plook'* is the nearest Scots equivalent to a 'wen'. *Sawnie:*   Alexander: e.g. *Sawnie Bean* is a corruption of *'Sawnie Bain':* Fair Alexander, and has nothing to do with English 'bean'. *cockernonie:* a bonnet or snood. *philabeg:* the small-kilt, as worn today. (Gaelic: *feile beag).Piskie:* A Scottish Episcopalian. *Jamie Saxt:* James VI of Scotland who became James I of England also. *thirled:* attached. *crannreuch:* hoar frost. *mirk:* dark, obscure. *blate:* shy. *stell:* support, hold up. *sheuch:* a ditch. *scunner: disgust (n.), to cause disgust (v.).* *theek:* thatch. *thole:* endure.

186

THE JOLLY TRIMMERS

or

LOVE OF SLAVERY.

A SATIRICAL CANTATA

IN SAD MEMORY OF, AND WITH APOLOGIES
TO, THAT GREAT BARD, REBEL, AND TRUE
SCOT,

ROBERT BURNS.

RECITATIVO

When Januar crannreuch bites the taes
and bodies seek the ingle's bleeze
or some mair modern lowe;
when warmit howffs are socht oot maist
and toddie's mair tae ilka taste
tae wames baith cauld and howe.....
sic nichts when blests of Januar wun
remind us aw o Rabbie
an set the bardic saul tae spin
oot dauds o Standard Habbie;
wi tatties, an haggis
richt found fur usquebae
the thrissle, maun rissle
fur three hours on yae day.

Sic nichts ye'll find the Suppers stert,
the last dunt o the Scottish hert
aw smoort by London capers;
whaur honest chiels are aw gart think
and ithers come juist fur the drink
or hope tae mak The Papers.
'Tis there ye'll see amang the rest,
in siller studs an laces,
Big Mucklewame in tartans drest,
amang yon sonsie faces;
we speechin, and preachin
his view o Scotland's State,
he'll tell ye, an sell ye
gin ye wad tak his bait.

BIG MUCKLEWAME'S SONG.

A son of Mammon I and I tell you all no lie.....
for I could sell and buy every man in the room;
but I'll never be content with a gain of ten percent
and I bolster up the rent of reach roof that I own.
                          CHORUS: Lal de daudle etc.....

And although I made my pile between Kirkwall and Carlisle
it's many a long mile that I've left them behind;
I've a house in London Town and another further down
where the southern social graces are more to my mind.

Where to further suit my ends I have made a lot of friends
for a pile of money tends to attract such a bunch,
and I whisper to them words on the subject of the The Lords
when they're round my festive board or I treat them to lunch.

Our dear old Robert Burns, well enough he served our turns
and our great respect he earns for his verses of note:
we make Scottish noises here at the dead time of the year
but we really have no fear when it comes to the vote.

We can plumb the Scottish deeps with the haggis and the neaps
for we're certain that it keeps down all Scottish desires;
as a safety valve its best, for all sep'ratist unrest.....
and for me an annual test of our dear Scotlandshire.

RECITATIVO

He endit tae a roosan cheer
and stampin on the flair.....
and aw his freens wha'd cam tae hear
nou yelloched oot fur mair;
but Lady Mucklewame wis near
tae quaiten doun the rair.....
aw glitterin i her West End gear
she shovit back her chair.

LADY MUCKLEWAME'S SONG

My Dad was a climber, my Dad was no fool
for he paid all my fees to the Very Best School,
while I had good advice from both Mumsie and Daddie
to walk up the aisle with a well-heeled laddie.

Dear Mumsie made sure that I 'came out' in Town
in the hope that I'd catch some baronial clown,
but if chinless was tinless I'd never go steady
but look all around for a well-heeled laddie.

The very first cast hooked a penniless peer
who sponged on his title for most of the year;
but those who prize sturgeon above finnan haddie
must set home the gaff in a well-heeled laddie.

So despite the blue ichor that ran in his veins
I dumped my lean Duke for more affluent swains;
to rule his new Scottish estate I was ready,
so I tilted my cap at the Mucklewame laddie.

Now gillies and stalkers I have by the score,
for in the far north I find game birds galore
and bowers and scrapers to call me My Lady
in hopes of a smile from my well-heeled laddie.

So on our way Northwards we take it in turns
to pretend we love tartan and haggis and Burns.....
a poet who never had much of the ready.....
I'm much better off with my well-heeled laddie.

RECITATIVO

Toombodie gled tae get a bite
sat guzzlin et a lower table,
wi usquebae bambaizlit quite
as muckle o't as he was able
fair tozie wi a guid nicht's soakin
he thocht as weel tae gie a sang
nou that he didna care a docken
fur the graund folk he sate amang.

TOOMBODIE'S SONG.

Auld Scotia's the land o my birth
Auld Scotland's the name o my nation;
thought I've daunnert across the wide Earth
I never hae felt sic frustration,
as when I cam back tae my hame
an saw whit the fowk there had made o't
a kintra that's no worth the name
that my noble forefathers yince laid on't.
Braid Scots wes the leid that I spak
on the day that I left the dockside;
in Gaelic I learnt hou tae crack
when I leeved my auld mither beside.

But nou it's become Scotland*sheer*
(fur yon is the wey they pronounce it)
there's nae ither leid that I hear
than 'pan-loaf' and I hereby renounce it;
nou they tak the auld leids frae the bairns
in the interests of standardisation.....
fur the elders they aw lack the harns
that formerly marked oot the nation.

But wha is there wad listen tae me
wha speak the auld leids o the land;
fur they arna the tongue o T.V.
or yon Oxbridge-cum-Westminster band.

An nou ilka speug that I hear
cheepin oot in oor high public places.....
Ah, Rabbie, ye're faur better there,
whaur ye're lowsit fra sic airs and graces.

RECITATIVO

Tae claim their lugs cam neist a lady
in tartan sash and Hielant cadie
nae crofter wes her husband's daddie
but fain he'd be a Hieland laddie;
Though Eton was his Alma Mater
he'd got ten million frae his pater,
and sae wi attitudes colonial
he chieftain'd it in Scotch Baronial.

THE SONG OF THE NEW LAIRD'S LADY.

A highland chief my love would be.....
the fashion in Society;
he purchased to impress his friends
a fortress in the lonely glens.

CHORUS:
Sing hey my new John Hielandman
Sing ho my new John Hielandman
For London Glossies now they stand
and pose round my John Hielandman.

Wi private tartan kilt an plaid
in Edinboro neatly made,
he makes wee birdies fear the gun
o my synthetic Hielandman.

Though west of Spey and north of Forth
of Hieland laddies there's a dearth,
these empty spaces suit the plan
of such as my John Hielandman.

They say they went across the sea
and left the place to John and me;
for miles and miles the moors you'll scan
and scarcely see a Highlandman.

But on the Twelfth the local poor
creep out from cairns to beat the moor
though Gaelic chatter then we ban.....
it much annoys my Hielandman. (†)

And after all the birds are shot
the London gourmets eat the lot;
the moor's deserted once again
for me and my John Hielandman

(†) *Beaters were sometimes reproved for speaking Gaelic.*

RECITATIVO

Straucht up there stood a pigmy pedant
wha et nit-pickin skeels was eident
he could bambaizle ilka bejant
wi's share of lear,
't was aw his walth and he wes gled on't
and gart thaim hear.....

We een fast shut and finger raisit
ilk southron scribblers wark he praisit
while his puir bejants blate and dazit
soaked up his sermon;
the native wark he thocht debasit.....
their scrievers vermin.

THE PEDANT'S SONG.
Tho bred tae speak the Scottish tongue
I smoort it oot when I wes young
but whether spoken wards or sung
I whustle owre the lave o't.

I am a pedant tae my trade.
tho Scottish born I'm southron made;
what if a traitor game I've played
I whustle owre the lave o't.

In lectures and in seminars
at parties or in city bars,
I find the Scottish language jars
and whustle ower the lave o't.

O coorse, the bardies o the past,
deep in their lang-hame yirdit fast
o thaim I shaw my learning vast
but whustle owre the lave o't.

RECITATIVO

At yon a sturdy artisan
wha'd got an invitation
fur gien the Club a helpin hand
(tho faur abune his station)
the pedant heized by the lapel
an thocht it richt tae heid him.....
syne that the wey he spak himsel
wes as his forebears gied him.

The pedant made shift tae appease
this king o square and level
and said he had but tried tae please
the ithers in the revel.
He winked his ee aboot the ring
and said the man wes fleein
when up the callant raise tae sing
in accents maist plebeian.

THE JOURNEYMAN'S SONG.

My maisters aw, sae bien and braw,
I am a bonie worker,
wi bolt or nail I never fail
tae shaw I am nae shirker;
I've sairved my time in monie a clime
an airned my keep richt brawlie
but nou I'm hame I win nae fame
whaur sma men aye misca me.

Wi my ain nieve ma skeel I'll preive
gin ye'll pit wark afore me;
yince, ilka tide upon the Clyde
there's no a man could waur me
yince, Scottish maisters fee'd my haund
an peyed me Scottish siller
but I maun seek some fremit land
when London hauds the tiller.

RECITATIVO

Anither had been listin there
but silent at his cup;
wha cam tae be at this affair
in hopes of bite and sup:
weel read in aw his kintra's lear
baith leids o't in his grup
no gart by favour or by fear
he thocht tae steer thaim up
wi's sang that nicht.

Frae Deorsa til the Book o Deer (†)
frae Hughie til the Dean (§)
there was nae word o Scottish lear
but that oor bard had seen;
weel could he thole the bitter sneer
the jag o envie's preen;
frae siccan chiels as didna care
tae tak a Scottish lean,
in sang that nicht.

Tho critics seenil sang his praise
an rare his publication,
the Scottish saul he saucht tae raise
tae pride in our auld nation.
He wisna like tae take the bays
for siccan exhortation,
nou Scotland does as England says
withooten altercation.
Ilk day and nicht.

THE BARD'S SONG.

There's nane regard me as bard
in smairt reviews and aw that;
braid Scots or Erse houever terse
it's doggerel they ca that
CHORUS.
For aw that and aw that
In English Lit. and aw that,
they'd raither chance a Pink Romance
than ocht in Scots and aw that

The 'in-crowd' bank in serried rank
fur Gaelic bards and aw that,
but whether damns they hear or psalms
they've nae idea fur aw that.

Tho Chaucer's strains they teach the weans
the southron bards and aw that,
puir Henryson will no get dune,
he's ower Scotch fur aw that.

Oor guid braid Scots, suburban lots
will caa it 'slang' and aw that:
an dominies will tak their fees
fur German, French and aw that.

When Jaik and Jill depairt the schuil
they yaise sic lear and aw that
for Moliere beside the fire
and Holderlin an aw that.

An yince a year, (nae mair, I fear)
in Scottish schools it's law that
the weans tak turns reciting Burns.....
neist day they maunna daur that.

RECITATIVO

Sae sang the bard an in the room
the listeners were stricken doom
and kent na whit tae dae;
twa that were there, weel fed and beered
the rebel bard wad fain have cheered
gin yin had shawn the wey.
But maist of thaim luikt et their plate
tae hide their lowin chafts
frae yin wha nither bauch nor blate
had lowsed at thaim sic shafts.
He rising, surprised them
we words baith bauld and braisant
a joyful disciple
o yon great Ayrshire peasant.

THE POET'S FINALE.

Who believe the Scottish nation
is of old and noble seed;
must with others take up station,
equal but no 'lesser breed'.
CHORUS:
All around the trimmers coax you
to despise a Scottish stance
all around the placemen hoax you
lead you in their party dance.

Some for wealth and some for title
some for place or private plan
would your native instincts bridle,
mould you to a lesser man.

Listen to our native voices
faint enough though they may be;
you'll be offered louder choices
fading when they've made you pay.

Cast an eye round moor and city
in our dowie Scottish land;
slum and larach get no pity
Scottie's robbed on every hand.

The daftest bairn knows rule by strangers
smothers out the native will;
family firms have lesser dangers,
family fingers in the till.

Night and day the trimmers wangle
add, subtract, the placemen know,
how to cover every angle,
keep daft Scottie down below.

> CHORUS:
> All around the trimmers coax you
> to despise a Scottish stance;
> all around the placemen hoax you
> lead you in their party dance.

crannreuch: frost. *lowe:* glow. *howffs:* pubs. *ilka:* each.
wames: stomachs. *Standard Habbie:* a Scots verse metre.
usquebae: whisky (uisge beatha). *thrissle:* thistle. *rissle:* rustle.
dunt: beat. *chiel:* fellow. *gart:* compelled to. *sonsie:* jolly.
gin (hard 'g'): if. *yelloched:* roared. *bambaizlit:* bamboozled.
tozie: tipsy. *daunnert:* wandered. *leid:* language.
crack: converse. *pan-loaf:* affected speech. *harns:* brains.
speug: sparrow. *cadie:* bonnet. *bejant:* first year student in a
Scottish University. *blate:* timid. *scriever:* writer. *whustle owre
the lave o't:* the rest can go hang. *yirdit:* buried. *heized:* hauled up.
syne: since. *fleein:* blind drunk. *bien and braw:* comfy and pretty.
nieve: fist. *preive:* prove. *fremit:* alien. *preen:* pin.
siccan: such. *seenil:* seldom. *ocht:* anything. *bauch:* sheepish.
lowin chafts: blushing cheeks. *braisant:* bold. *dowie:* sad.
larach: ruin of a former dwelling.

(†) Deorsa Mac Iain Deorsa: the by-name of the late George Campbell
Hay. *The Book of Deer* is the earliest Scottish Gaelic document.
(§) The Book of the Dean is a collection of Gaelic poetry compiled in the
sixteenth century.